MW01017339

IT'S A JUNGLE AT HOME

Debra White Smith

HARVEST HOUSE PUBLISHERS

EUGENE, OREGON

All Scripture quotations are taken from the HOLY BIBLE, NEW INTERNATIONAL VERSION®. NIV®. Copyright © 1973, 1978, 1984 by the International Bible Society. Used by permission of Zondervan. All rights reserved.

Debra White Smith: Published in association with the literary agency of Alive Communications, Inc., 7680 Goddard Street, Ste #200, Colorado Springs, CO 80920.

Every effort has been made to give proper credit for all stories, poems, and quotations. If for any reason proper credit has not been given, please notify the author or publisher and proper notation will be given on future printing.

Cover by Koechel Peterson & Associates, Inc., Minneapolis, Minnesota

Cover photo: Tom Henry/Koechel Peterson & Associates, Inc.

IT'S A JUNGLE AT HOME

Copyright © 2006 by Debra White Smith
Published by Harvest House Publishers
Eugene, Oregon 97402
www.harvesthousepublishers.com

Library of Congress Cataloging-in-Publication Data

Smith, Debra White.
   It's a jungle at home / Debra White Smith.
      p. cm.
   Includes bibliographical references.
   ISBN-13: 978-0-7369-1057-6 (pbk.)
   ISBN-10: 0-7369-1057-3
   1. Parent and child—Religious aspects—Christianity. 2. Parent and child—Humor. 3. Parenting—Religious aspects—Christianity. 4. Parenting—Humor. I. Title.
   BV4529.S478 2006
   248.8'431—dc22
                                                                                    2005019222

Printed in the United States of America

06 07 08 09 10 11 12 13 14 / VP-MS / 10 9 8 7 6 5 4 3 2 1

For my mother—
Sorry about that shampoo in the hallway!

Contents

1

Alligators in My Pantry

*There is a time for everything and a season for
every activity under heaven.*

ECCLESIASTES 3:1

Hello, my name is Debra, and I'm a closet slob. My idea of closet management involves opening the door, closing my eyes, tossing in whatever needs to go inside, and slamming the door before anything falls out on me. My kitchen pantry is a prime example of how my system works. Often when I open my pantry door, food falls out at my feet. All sorts of odds and ends. Elbow macaroni. Cooking oil. Walnuts. Baking mix…that of course is always open and releases a powdery dash of white across my needs-to-be-mopped floor. But that doesn't bother me. *No sir-ee!* I've learned to just step over that mess and keep digging through the shelves for that lone chocolate bar stuck in the far back corner of the pantry since 1970.

Any time my husband opens the pantry door and food falls out at his feet, I hear him squawk, "She booby-trapped me again!" How could he be so paranoid? Does the man actually think I have time to booby trap him? No way! Not with chasing after two kids and a full-blown writing and speaking ministry. Sometimes I think the man has gone nuts.

Actually, there has been a time or two when I almost went nuts trying to find some remotely used spice, such as salt for instance, shoved against the back wall. Once, after all my scrounging and scavenging, I wondered if perhaps wildlife might start growing in my pantry. You know, harmless critters like alligators or water moccasins. Then I reminded myself that those reptiles need water. And while my pantry certainly supplies plenty of wilderness territory, there is no water. Okay, I have found swamps of spilled syrup that dripped off one shelf, streamed down the wall in elegant amber rivulets, and formed a graceful puddle on the shelf below. But I cleaned that up.

What's so hilarious about all this is that before I had kids, I was an immaculate housekeeper. Well, my pantry and closets have never been perfect, but they were certainly better than they are now. B.C. (before children) I used to be *soooo* judgmental about my friends who had kids. I'd go over to a friend's house and think, *I don't know why she can't keep her house cleaner than this!* Then I had kids! And suddenly I couldn't figure out why I could never get my house to look as good as my friends' who had children.

For awhile I really struggled with guilt over the state of my once-pristine home. But finally I realized that the only way I was ever going to have a spotless house again was if I turned into a cleaning she-devil. You know, a mama who carries a whip in one hand and a broom in the other and wields her Windex with a split-second precision that would put most gunslingers to shame.

I've come to the conclusion that I'd rather have a relaxed, happy atmosphere in my home than an uptight existence that doesn't allow my children to be children. No, the floors aren't spotless. And honestly, I did just scrub something from my toilets that looked like it came off the creature from the black lagoon. Furthermore, I have wondered a time or two if whole subcultures were growing on top of my refrigerator. But I've got two happy children who fling themselves into my arms and say, "You're the best mama in the universe!"

One day these little guys are going to go off to college and leave me with all the time in the world. Then I'll alphabetize my canned goods and organize my closet according to wardrobe color scheme. And the whole time, I'm sure I'll be wailing for the days when I wondered if there were alligators in my pantry.

SURVIVAL SKILL

Any time you have a bag of chips or box of crackers with only a few left, go ahead and throw them away. It's a known scientific fact that all nearly empty bags and boxes crawl to the back of the pantry at midnight and entrench themselves for decades.

If you have to choose between taking the time to allow God to keep your heart spotless and taking the time to keep your house spotless, always choose a spotless heart.

2

Maxi-Cat

A wife of noble character who can find? She is
worth far more than rubies.

PROVERBS 31:10

After a trip to the grocery store, I was coming in the front door with my two children. At the time, Brett and Brooke were five and three respectively. I walked through the front door, followed by Brett, then Brooke. Brooke is a pint-sized force who is quite accomplished at slamming the door. She whacked the door shut.

Unfortunately, our cat, Mamma Kitty, seems to have this fatal attraction to slamming doors. She was just stepping outside at the same time the door banged. Often her tail is the injured appendage. This time the door smashed her back paw. Mamma Kitty screeched and ran to the top step outside. Brett and I joined Brooke and the cat to see that the cat's paw was bleeding rather profusely.

Brett, being the high-strung variety, started screaming, "The kitty's bleeding, Mama! She's bleeding! She's bleeding!" He paused for some sobs.

Brooke produced some worried sounds, and Mamma Kitty somehow ran back into the house. All I could think was that the cat was going to track blood all over my hardwood floors and faux oriental rugs. So we all followed the cat indoors, and I scooped her up.

"She needs a Band-Aid," one of the kids said.

I agreed. I took the bleeding cat to the bathroom, put her in the bathtub, and closed the shower door. She was now meowing, deeply disturbed, and tracking blood all over the bathtub. After a brief search for a Band-Aid, I remembered we were out.

Have you ever noticed how all children under the age of eight think Band-Aids are the cure for everything from warts to cancer? I recalled that Brett and Brooke had gotten into the Band-Aid box and plastered them on their bodies, on the floor, here, there, and everywhere.

Since we were out of bandages, I was going to have to make one. Brett was still sobbing over the kitty's paw, and Brooke was silently contemplating the scene. I decided that the second best thing to a Band-Aid was toilet paper and packing tape. So I raced to my office in search of packing tape, until I remembered I'd run out.

I went back to the restroom, seriously considering my options. Brett stood in my bedroom, all uptight and fretting. Brooke, the cat-slayer, still silently observed. I believe in divine consultation in every area of my life, so I said, "I think we need to pray for our kitty."

"I already did that!" Brett wailed. The cat was still howling in the bathtub. "She needs a Band-Aid!" Brett insisted.

At that point I experienced one of those rare moments of genius. An idea began on the horizon of my mind, gradually took shape, and eventually turned into the answer to all my problems. I didn't have any Band-Aids, but I did have a maxi-pad. I rushed into the bathroom, reached into the cabinet, and grabbed one of them.

"What's that, Mama?" Brooke asked.

"It's a special Band-Aid," I said.

As the cat continued howling, I unwrapped the maxi-pad and unfolded it.

"It sure is a big one," Brett said.

"Yes it is," I agreed and stifled the burst of hilarity pressing upon me.

Before long I had the cat on the bathroom counter. I attempted to wrap that maxi-pad around her paw. Well, let's just say that a maxi-pad was not meant to serve as a Band-Aid for a cat's paw. No matter how hard I tried, I just couldn't get it to work. Hoping for the best, I finally decided to put the poor cat outside so she wouldn't traipse blood all over my house. In a few hours, you could hardly tell that the cat had experienced a traumatic morning.

Later I remembered something highly significant in the midst of all that cat howling. When I suggested that we pray for the cat, Brett, at the ripe old age of five, had said, "I already did that." Even in the middle of domestic chaos, Brett immediately turned to God as a source of help without any urging from me. As the woman who is honored to be his mother, I was quite blessed.

Could it be that the little boy who prayed for his kitty's smashed paw had been influenced by the woman he had seen starting each day with prayer and Bible reading?

Mom, do you know just how powerful and influential you are in your family? Proverbs 31:10 says, "A wife of noble character, who can find? She is worth far more than rubies." In the Hebrew, the word for "noble character" is the same one used in the Bible for army. It means a force, whether of men, means, or other resources; an army, wealth, virtue, valor, strength, substance, worthy. According to Barna Research group, 78 percent of teens say their parents, and especially their mothers, have considerable influence in their thinking and behavior.[1] Never underestimate your powerful presence in your home!

SURVIVAL SKILL

Don't give small children Band-Aids for anything except real wounds oozing real blood. Otherwise they will use them all in a matter of days, and when you actually need them, you won't have them.

The only thing more powerful than talking to God
is being still and listening to God…
and then actually doing what He says.

3

Some People Are Soooo Picky!

*She considers a field and buys it; out of her earnings
she plants a vineyard. She sets about her work vigorously;
her arms are strong for her tasks. She sees that her trading
is profitable, and her lamp does not go out at night.*

PROVERBS 31:16-18

When you are a mom who runs a home-based ministry or business, you may have the delightful chore of managing both business and personal checking accounts. Presently, I manage our personal account, two business accounts, and our family's investments. For the most part, I keep up with the accounts without a problem. But occasionally I really pull off a whopper of an error.

Several years ago I deposited a check for $4,000 into my and my husband's joint account. Then I wrote a $4,000 check to a credit-card company out of one of our business accounts. Unfortunately, the business account did not have $4,000 in it. And would you believe the bank had the audacity to bounce that check? Some people are soooo picky!

I realized my mistake when I received an overdraft notice from the bank. Being the responsible sort, I called the credit-card company and asked them if they'd received the check back. They had not. I explained what had happened and asked them to just discard the check. I told them I'd mail another one. I immediately did so.

Meanwhile, the credit-card company somehow got my message twisted and thought they were supposed to run the original check back through my checking account. When they did, the check bounced again. So I called the credit-card company and explained my sad, sorry story all over again. The representative was very understanding and profusely apologized. Nevertheless, shortly thereafter I received a letter from the credit-card company telling me they'd canceled my credit card.

So I called the credit-card company again and had the privilege of speaking to a third representative who, like her predecessors, had no history of my lengthening saga. By this time, the company had received my new payment and that check had cleared. When I told my yarn for the third time, the representative said, "This sounds like a comedy of errors." From that point on, I knew I'd connected with someone who had a *clue*. What a concept! This lady cleared up everything and reissued my credit card.

I don't think a day goes by that I don't make a mistake of some sort. Thankfully, most of my errors aren't the $4,000 variety. Many of them are the equivalent of nickels or dimes. Sometimes, I'll pull off a whopper that would gain a $1,000 to $3,000 score. Those are the days I refer to as "bad days." And if the mistake involves my kids, it's a "really bad day."

There's not a woman on the planet who hasn't made some $4,000 mistakes, whether in finances, career or ministry choices, or parenting. Even though the rest of the world might not understand our blunders, God is much like the third credit-card representative. He has a *clue!* As a matter of fact, He has *all* the clues! He has the answers to our money problems, business problems, marriage problems, and parenting problems. Anytime I'm in the throes of beating myself up for my own mistakes, the Lord is always there with support, forgiveness, and a heart full of unconditional love.

SURVIVAL SKILL

Arrange for overdraft protection on your checking accounts, and keep your business checks in a different color cover than your personal checks. That way you're less likely to grab the wrong one. But there are no guarantees when the kids are screaming!

Any time I'm tempted to criticize someone,
I remind myself of two important truths:
Nobody's perfect and everyone makes mistakes.
That includes me!

4

The "Perfect Moms" Club

But my dove, my perfect one, is unique.

SONG OF SONGS 6:9

One of the things our family loves to do is go to Six Flags Over Texas in Dallas. When I step into the gates of that amusement park, I embrace the whole scene. I love the rides, the smells, and the adventure. I wouldn't deprive my kids of one minute of the whole experience.

The second we begin our journey, my kids (now nine and eleven) start hopping up and down like a couple of kangaroos. "Can we ride the Texas Chute Out? Can we ride Judge Roy's Scream? I want some cotton candy…and a Pink Thing! Oh, and a candy apple too! Look… let's do the log ride first!" They grab my husband and me by the hands and pull us forward. But they don't have to pull too hard. We're nearly as eager as they are.

If everything goes as usual, by five o'clock I've been flipped upside down, whipped around and around, dropped from the sky, flung over roller coaster hills, splashed, dunked, and knocked nearly flat by a wall of water otherwise known as Splashwater Falls. Nearly every scrap of makeup I put on that morning has been scared off my face, and the few traces that are left are rearranged. When I dare look in the mirror, I see mascara flakes hanging to my chin, blusher that looks striped, and lipstick smudges in places that should be illegal. My shirt may have a mustard stain. My shorts are crumpled. And my feet and socks are so wet they feel like wadded up strips of leather.

The last time we went to Six Flags, my son started complaining about his feet after we'd ridden enough water rides to drown a whale. Our family plopped on some park benches and decided it would behoove us all to remove our shoes and socks. When we did, we recognized that our feet could easily be mistaken for pale prunes—especially my son's. Poor little guy! He'd *really* enjoyed those water rides.

Early in our feet conversation, I became aware that we had plunked ourselves down beside one of "those" women. You know the kind I mean. The ones who look like they are the founders of The "Perfect Moms" Club—that ever-elusive body of women who do everything right. They even arrive at Six Flags in strappy sandals, perfectly hairsprayed hair, makeup in all the right places, and cute linen shorts just the right length to modestly expose their lack of cellulite. So there she sat with her little one—a male child about seven years old. He too looked neat and well-pressed. And there I sat with my rearranged makeup airing my pruned feet.

My motto in life is and always has been, if somebody's within six feet of me, then they need to be talked to. So I struck up a conversation. I said something really brilliant like, "We've been on a lot of water rides." She smiled and replied with something clever. I continued to chat, all the while wishing I could tell her that I looked a little like her "in a former life"—as in that morning around nine.

By that point, my son joined the conversation. He shares my life motto about talking to people. So in graphic detail he began to describe our day to this founder of The "Perfect Moms" Club. He shared that he and I had ridden Judge Roy's Scream—that sling-you-batty roller coaster—three times in a row, and that his mom had actually stood with him to get slammed by a wall of water. I stopped caring about my droopy hair, rumpled clothes, and flaky mascara. In the light of his glowing eyes and animated face, I realized that that day I was my son's hero. I didn't have to feel inferior to any perfect mom out there. Despite how I looked, I was perfect to him.

Many times in the New Testament when the word "perfect" is used in relationship to people, it does not mean without flaws. The word means "able to be fully used for what it was created for." Essentially, the word "complete" best describes the original meaning. God created each of us for many unique purposes.

One of those purposes for me is being a mom to my children. I'm the only woman on the planet who can do that in my special way. And while I doubt anyone will ever ask me to join The "Perfect Moms" Club, one day I'll be able to look back and say my attempts were complete…and quite fulfilling.

SURVIVAL SKILL

The best hair spray I've found is Big, Sexy Hair. While it will not hold up under a wall of water, that stuff will keep your hair put all day, even in wind; and it doesn't look heavy. But it's expensive. When my budget is tight, there are times when I use a cheap brand of hair spray for around the house and save the good stuff for when I'm going to be seen by the rest of the world.

*You can have perfect hair, makeup,
and shoes when your kids are grown.
Between now and then,
enjoy the prune-feet moments.*

5

French Fry Flambé

I have been reminded of your sincere faith,
which first lived in your grandmother
Lois and in your mother Eunice and,
I am persuaded, now lives in you also.
For this reason I remind you to fan into flame
the gift of God, which is in you
through the laying on of my hands.

2 TIMOTHY 1:5

French fries are an American institution. My children are definitely American; they love fries. Since I lean more toward being a health nut, I often bake crinkle fries or tater tots for the kids. But about once a month, I still fry them up a big pan of french fries. Admittedly, I love the crunch of a crisp fry just as much as any kid.

Several years ago, I filled an iron skillet full of cooking oil and piled the french fries in the skillet. I noticed I'd gotten the skillet a little full, but I decided to do the best I could with the situation. In the middle of the frying, I stepped into my home office for but a moment. Still focused upon my cooking, I returned to the stove within a minute or two—only to discover my fries were flaming! My over-filled pan of fries had leaked oil onto the burner. Yellow, red, and blue flames engulfed the pan.

I experienced a flashback to my childhood. During a family movie, my mother placed a pan with oil in it on the stove. She stepped out of the kitchen with plans to return and prepare popcorn once the oil was hot. Unfortunately, she got involved in the movie, forgot the pan, and the whole thing caught on fire. My father had grabbed a potholder, grasped the pan's handle, and hurtled toward the back door. He tossed the pan into the yard. The flames immediately stopped. I tried to imagine myself mimicking my dad, but I couldn't get past the image of my spilling the fries and oil all over the floor and possibly catching the kitchen on fire.

Then I remembered the fire extinguisher. We'd been required to have one in the kitchen for our home's adoption inspection. Once I retrieved that long red canister from the wall hanger, I was faced with another problem: How to operate it! With the flames gaining fervor, I prodded and pulled and gouged at the various appendages on the fire extinguisher.

Finally, as a last resort, I decided to read the fine print near the top of the extinguisher. After pushing this button and pulling that lever, I was able to press the trigger and receive significant results. A white blast erupted from the nozzle. The fire disappeared. I turned off the burner, pulled the hot pan to a cool spot, and examined the french fries. What once promised to be a crisp treat was now a batch of soggy, gray, gooey potato strips.

By this point, my husband had heard the seconds-long upheaval and rushed to the kitchen. "What happened?" he asked.

"I caught a pan of french fries on fire," I explained, still holding the fire extinguisher.

He eyed the extinguisher, the yucky pan of fries, then me. "Are you okay?"

"Yes," I said and continued with something like, "I'm the sharpest shooter in the south."

He chuckled and said, "We won't be eating these, will we?"

"No." I sighed and considered the empty fries bag in the trash can. "And I don't have any more either. I guess I'll have to plan some other vegetable for dinner."

While Daniel hung up the fire extinguisher, I dumped the pan of fries outside and congratulated myself on dealing with the crisis in a timely and sensible manner—even if I did have to read the instructions to work the fire extinguisher.

Statistics show that a significant number of serious house fires start in the kitchen, often due to a situation just like mine and my mom's. The chef on duty steps out of the kitchen for just a second and either forgets that pan of oil on the burner or just misses the moment when the fire ignites.

The fire in our souls is much different from the fires in our kitchen. Interestingly enough, while stepping away from a cooking meal might result in spontaneous combustion, stepping away from seriously pursuing the Lord will result in a cold heart. Surveys show that many moms don't take the time to keep the fire burning in their souls. While having a fire in our kitchen is a far cry from "safe," having a holy inferno in our hearts is exactly what moms need. A mother with a passionate relationship with Jesus Christ is more likely to hear His voice when a parenting crisis is on. I've found that the closer I walk to Christ, the more likely I am to keep a cool head, even if I'm tired and the kids are grumpy.

Like many moms, I've struggled with how to make time in my hectic day for an encounter with the Lord. Sometimes I think we set ourselves up for failure by thinking if we don't get up at six o'clock in the morning, light a candle, put on a choir robe, and listen to organ music, we just aren't spiritual enough. The problem with being a mom—especially of young children—is that the nature of the job involves the unexpected. The very day you do manage to get up at six for prayer will be the day a sleepy-eyed toddler arrives at your side and, without a word, throws up all over you and the floor. So there you are, mopping vomit, when you're scheduled to be praying.

When my kids were younger, out of desperation I finally asked God to give me time every day when I could stoke the fire in my soul. He answered my prayer. Nearly every day my kids would unexpectedly conk out in front of the TV while I was preparing a snack. Like any other industrious mom, I saw the break as an opportunity to straighten the house or do the dishes. But the second I stepped toward the pile of dishes in the sink, I would hear a still small voice beckoning me to sit in the presence of the Lord rather than scrub pots and pans. So I'd leave the dishes until later and snuggle down in the couch with my Bible and a heart ready to absorb God's Spirit and wisdom. Amazingly, I always found time to do the dishes later.

Many nights, one of my children would awaken for any number of reasons and need me in the wee hours. After my child went back to sleep, I'd think, *I haven't had a serious prayer time in a couple of days. I've already been awake an hour. Another hour won't hurt me.* And I'd get my Bible, put on my worship music, and encounter God.

For me, encountering God means I take the time to fall silent and listen for His voice in the recesses of my soul. Sometimes I need help in solving parental issues. Or I wait for the Lord to give me insights for my writing and speaking. On other occasions, I lift up issues with people or difficult decisions. Sure it's important to bring my requests to Him...and I do. But waiting for the Lord's guidance and basking in the warmth of His presence are just as important as talking to Him. This allows prayer time to be a dynamic, two-way communication, rather than a one-person monologue.

It's so easy to develop a McDonald's mentality with God. We often approach Him like we would place an order at a fast-food window. "Hey, God, give me an extra large order of blessings and smear on some ketchup, will Ya?" Then we zoom right through our day and never take the time to allow Him to stoke the fire in our souls. Just as good moms are committed to spending quality time with their kids, so we need to commit to spending quality time with the Lord.

Remember to show your children the image of a godly mother. The more spiritually minded you are, the more likely they are to be spiritual teens and adults. Don't make excuses for neglecting God. The colder your heart grows, the less likely you are to hear the voice of the Lord, and the more mistakes you will make as a parent.

SURVIVAL SKILL

> If you don't have a kitchen fire extinguisher, you can get one in the hardware department of many stores. If you have one, make sure you know how to work it!

You're the only one who can choose
to allow God to stoke the fire in your soul.

6

Peanut Gooey

Let the little children come to me, and do not hinder them,
for the kingdom of God belongs to such as these.

MARK 10:14

One fall I purchased a big bag of peanuts with a yummy-sounding peanut brittle recipe on the back of the bag. When I showed the peanuts to my kids, I said, "We're going to make peanut brittle!" They were delighted, and we began to plan a time in our schedule when we could create the best peanut brittle of the century.

At long last the magic moment arrived. Brooke, still too short to cook without a stool, stood on her kitchen ladder while Brett hovered close. Like normal siblings, they argued over who got to put in the sugar and syrup. Once I convinced them to take turns adding ingredients, they argued over who went first. Finally we got all the ingredients into the boiler and carefully added the peanuts when the recipe said.

According to this recipe, we were supposed to cook the peanuts in the mixture for about 20 minutes. Honestly, that seemed a little odd to me, but since I've never actually made peanut brittle, I figured I should go with what the recipe said. After all, it was on the back of the bag.

After the appropriate time had lapsed, we prepared our pan for the brittle by spraying it with olive oil. Then we added the baking soda to the brittle and enjoyed the sight of the mixture foaming like an erupting volcano. With great glee we poured the mixture into the pan and watched as all the fizz evaporated, leaving a graying goo in its wake.

I don't know what the kids were thinking at that point, but I must admit I had my doubts. The longer the mixture sat in the pan, the weirder it looked. The concoction was an odd shade of grayish-brown. I've never seen that exact color before or since. I kept testing the dessert, expecting it to at least start hardening, but it stayed in a limbo state of extra gooey.

Finally my husband walked through the kitchen. He's the "dessert king" around our house and is usually the one who makes the sweets. He said, "Oooh. That doesn't look quite right."

"Yeah, I know," I replied and grabbed a spoon. I lifted one corner of the peanut-infested swamp substance and had a sudden surge of optimism. "I'm sure it will harden soon," I said. "After supper, it ought to be just right."

Silently he raised his brows and meandered along.

Soon supper was served, eaten, and forgotten. I don't have a clue what we had for the meal that night, but I'll never forget the peanut brittle. Let's just say that in order to eat the stuff, we had to dip it out with a spoon. My son experimented with a generous portion of the peanut gooey mixture and declared it was good, even though he labored to chew his first bite. I tried it and realized the stuff was at least good for pulling fillings from cavities—or maybe even a super glue substitute, if you didn't mind the bumpy peanuts in whatever you were trying to cement together!

At this point, my husband spoke up. Now understand that Daniel is a kind, soft-spoken gentleman who reaps the admiration of many—including me. However, he was moving fast that night, and his green eyes were sparkling with a determination I'm not sure I have ever seen in him before.

"I think it might be a good idea for you to call Joe's wife," he said, a hint of desperation in his upbeat suggestion.

"Joe's wife?" I asked.

"Yes. You know, Joe, who recently retired from work." He nodded with encouragement.

"Yes," I said and wondered exactly where he was going with this little suggestion.

"Well, every year, his wife brought the *best* peanut brittle I've ever

eaten. It was gold and light and crunchy." He didn't say, "Just the opposite of this goo you just cooked." And, well, it's probably a good thing!
Any man who ever makes such a suggestion to his wife better make
sure every expression is innocent and serene. It also doesn't hurt to
bend on one knee and bestow a gentle kiss upon the backs of each
hand after offering the advice.

But frankly, Daniel didn't even give me time to consider calling
Joe's wife or getting miffed or worried that he was not on bended knee.
No siree! Before you could say "peanut brittle," he had called Joe, made
his request, and had Joe's wife on the phone for me. After all, desperate
times call for desperate measures.

Soon I held the recipe for golden peanut brittle that tastes like it
came from heaven's very own candy store. Before hanging up, I shared
the other recipe with Joe's wife, and she and I decided the instructions
must have been written incorrectly on the bag. Fortunately, my husband readily agreed that my culinary abilities could have *never* been to
blame!

A day or two after I held that recipe in my hands, the kids and I
repeated our efforts in the kitchen—this time with grand success!
When my husband wandered through the kitchen and witnessed us
pouring the golden mixture into the pan, he nodded his approval and
said, "Now you're going to see a difference in this!" as if he were the
decade's prime authority on peanut brittle.

And guess what? He was right! That peanut brittle hardened in no
time, and we were all swooning in rapture.* That phone call Daniel
placed was nothing short of divine intervention!

Sometimes in life, we may think we're doing the right thing, but
like my first peanut brittle recipe, we may be following the wrong
instructions. Wrong instructions can come in the form of dysfunctional patterns passed down from one generation to the next, such as
perpetual yelling and griping. Or wrong instructions can come in the
form of parenting concepts based on isolated scriptures that support
unbalanced teaching or discipline over love. Such concepts usually
ignore the heart of Christ and place children as less important than
adults.

---

* **Note:** See recipe for this peanut brittle on page 205.

What mothering "instructions" are you living out? If you want to revolutionize your relationship with your kids, start with Jesus first. In Matthew 7:12, Jesus said, "So in everything, do to others what you would have them do to you." "Everything" means, well, everything. As mothers, it's our duty to never treat our children in a way we wouldn't want to be treated ourselves. This in no way means we don't discipline them. But even discipline should be carried out in a way that doesn't destroy the child's dignity.

Jesus said, "Let the little children come to me, and do not hinder them, for the kingdom of God belongs to such as these" (Mark 10:14). Christ Himself calls us to allow our children to come to Him. We hinder their advances toward Christ when we do not emulate Him in front of them and to them.

Just as my right recipe for peanut brittle produced dessert "art," so using the right recipe for raising our children will produce beautiful results. Jesus Christ is the author of the best child-rearing concepts available. His precepts start with unconditional love and acceptance. We need to incorporate these into our lives and be moms who are willing to treat our children the way we want to be treated.

SURVIVAL SKILL

Use an eraser to remove scuff marks on light-colored dress shoes.

Any time I've blown it with my kids,
I apologize to them, pray for God's forgiveness
in front of them, and take comfort in 1 Peter 4:8:
"Above all, love each other deeply,
because love covers over a multitude of sins."

7

Somebody Call the Cat Burglar

Listen, my son, to your father's instruction and do not forsake
your mother's teaching. They will be a garland to grace your head and a
chain to adorn your neck.

PROVERBS 1:8-9

When my son was a baby, we adopted a kitten whom we fondly dubbed "Meow Kitty" because Brett called him "Meow." Until Brett was four, he and Meow Kitty were best friends. One day we realized we hadn't seen Meow Kitty in a day or two. Having lived with cats my whole life, I immediately suspected the worst. Sure enough, we found Meow Kitty under a tree in our front yard. The second I saw him from a distance, I knew Meow Kitty was history. While Brett was disturbed, I soothed his pain with promises of getting another cat.

I went to the local animal shelter and picked out a gray striped kitten. I can't remember what we originally named the kitten, but her name evolved to Mamma Kitty after she gave birth to her first litter. I had purposefully allowed Mamma Kitty to give birth because I thought it would be an educational and fun experience for our children. Much to my husband's vexation, we kept all her kittens because we just couldn't bear to part with any of them.

However, those kittens grew up so fast I barely had time to blink. Without realizing it, I was soon "blessed" with a group of adult cats. During the time of their mating rituals, I was under a book deadline and didn't realize until it was too late that Mamma Kitty was going to be a grandmother very soon.

By April 2001, I was the proud owner of a whole herd of cats—nearly 20! I had six adult cats, two of which gave birth to kittens at the same time. My kids were elated. My husband was not a happy camper. I was dismayed. The two mama cats fought with each other over rights to the kittens. They both thought all the kittens belonged to them.

After a series of mishaps, natural disasters, and adoption scenarios, I was able to relieve our household of all the extra cats. I also proceeded to the vet and had each of the adult cats spayed or neutered. But for awhile, I was praying for a cat burglar.

One of the male cats had several names before we finally settled upon "Big Ol' Fat Daddy Cat." Big Ol' Fat Daddy Cat had a beautiful rich, gray coat with blue undertones. He was one of the most loving cats I've ever had. He was also *huge!* One of the names we called him for awhile was Goliath. I was on the verge of taking Big Ol' Fat Daddy Cat to the vet to have him neutered, but the very week I planned to set the appointment, Big Ol' Fat Daddy Cat came up missing. I assumed he must have fallen to the same fate as Meow Kitty.

However, within a few weeks, Big Ol' Fat Daddy Cat showed up in our backyard. He was now a scrawny, leery version of his former self. He went from an affectionate feline to a wild animal. Big Ol' Fat Daddy Cat would sit on the edge of the yard and watch us. When we tried to approach him, he ran. I told the kids if they ever caught him to holler, and we'd immediately put him in the cat carrier and take him to the vet to be relieved of his manhood.

But we never could catch him. Through the next three or four years, we'd see Big Ol' Fat Daddy Cat roaming our neighborhood, sometimes several streets away from our house. He gradually grew skinnier and started looking chewed up. He was on the streets, living the wild life. Still, every once in a while, we'd see Big Ol' Fat Daddy Cat eating out of the cat's bowl in our backyard. A few times we nearly caught him, but he always managed to escape.

Any time the feline would grace us with his presence, I'd tell the kids, "Big Ol' Fat Daddy Cat is living a wild life. He's not living right. Just look at him. Look how sad and sorry and chewed up he is. Look at Mamma Kitty. She's his mama. She's all nice and healthy because she's not out chasing around. This is what happens to people who go out and live a wild life. It starts taking its toll, and they're not healthy. They look bad and don't live as long. Remember, that's what drugs and alcohol do to you. Don't ever even go there."

One day I noticed Big Ol' Fat Daddy Cat was hanging around the house more than usual. He was still every bit as wild as he'd ever been, but he was looking worse. He was bone thin. He labored to breathe. His nose and eyes were matting with mucus. I knew that if Big Ol' Fat Daddy Cat didn't get some medical attention he could die. But as hard as I tried, I could not catch that cat.

One day when our family arrived home from a ministry trip, we opened our van doors and were greeted with the awful aroma of a rotting corpse. My husband found Big Ol' Fat Daddy Cat dead outside our bedroom window, near the back of our house. I took my children to my bedroom, opened the blinds, and said, "Just look at Big Ol' Fat Daddy Cat. Just look at him. He's dead. Do you know why he died? Big Ol' Fat Daddy Cat lived a wild life. He went out on the streets and chased girls and wouldn't stay home and behave. This is what happens to people who get involved in drugs and alcohol and who go out chasing around on the streets. Big Ol' Fat Daddy Cat did *not* have Jesus in his heart."

"Cats can't have Jesus in their hearts," the kids laughingly scoffed.

"No," I said, "but you can. And you do." I looked at Brett. "And you don't need to go chasing after girls."

Both the children laughed some more.

At that time, Brett was nine. Chasing girls was the last thing he had on his mind. But I know one day Brett will be seventeen, and girls will be the first thing on his mind. At some point, he and Brooke will most likely be offered cigarettes, drugs, or alcohol by one of their peers. As a mother, I'm trying to use everyday occasions to paint graphic pictures for them of what happens when they make wrong choices in life. I don't think either of my kids will ever forget smelling or seeing Big Ol' Fat Daddy Cat's decaying carcass. Neither do I anticipate their forgetting the things I told them about the consequences of his wrong choices.

SURVIVAL SKILL

Never give human painkillers to cats. They go into convulsions and die.

Wise mothers don't wait for formal settings
to teach their children.
They daily instruct their children in solid truths
using the fabric of everyday life as
ready-made object lessons.

8

Help!
My Refrigerator Is Possessed!

Get wisdom, get understanding.

PROVERBS 4:5

You know you're behind in the kitchen when you start thinking of doing dishes in terms of doing laundry...a load of plates...a load of forks...a load of cups. I've come to the conclusion that some of my dishes hop out of the cabinets while I sleep and fling themselves into the sink. There's no other explanation for the piles of dishes that never go away.

And then there's the actual laundry that just won't stop. Sometimes I think that while I'm putting socks in the washing machine they talk to each other. I imagine they're saying something like, "You go under the bed, and I'll go behind the dryer. Then she'll never match us up again. It will make her bananas!"

Once our washing machine malfunctioned. My husband, Daniel, is the mechanical sort so he tore into it. He'd never worked on a washing machine before but figured he could learn as he went. He was right. He had the thing working in no time.

In the process, he had to remove the tub. Guess what he found between the tub and the washing machine cavity? Socks! One of each of several socks we'd long ago thrown away because we were missing the mates. That day I learned a valuable lesson. Washing machines might look harmless, but in reality they are savage sock eaters. If your washing machine tub has an opening at the top, chances are high those socks you're missing are between the tub and the washing machine cavity.

And then there's the refrigerator. My refrigerator is possessed. That's the only explanation I can come up with. I can put perfectly good vegetables in there one day and in no time they're at the very back of the shelf growing mold. I think the minute I close the refrigerator door, two big arms emerge from the side walls and pull all the leftovers to the back so I can't find them. Then weeks later I stumble across some mashed potatoes dotted in this fungus-stuff that looks like it came off Mars.

And what is the deal with ceiling fans and light fixtures? Where *do* they collect all that dust from anyway? I promise, one summer day I turned off one of my ceiling fans, and it looked like it was growing fur! I told Daniel, "I think I'll skin the ceiling fan and make myself a fur coat!" He laughed.

Recently, when my friend and part-time housekeeper arrived, I asked her to clean the light fixtures and ceiling fans. That lone chore took hours, and JoAnn is a working machine! I'm seriously beginning to wonder if light fixtures *produce* dust. Maybe that's a by-product of the lighting process. It's like lightbulb pollen.

Honestly, there are some days I feel as if the dishes, dust, laundry, phone calls, and bills are burying me alive. Most busy moms feel exactly this way. I've learned to step over piles of laundry, ignore dishes in the sink, and turn the ceiling fan back on in a hurry so I don't have to look at the fur.

The deal is, there are only so many hours in the day and only one of me to go around. Can you relate? In order to survive, I usually start every day with a mental priority list. I know what I absolutely have to do that day and what is the most important. I do those things and don't sweat the stuff I can't get to. Some days the item on the top of my list is having a tea party with my daughter or taking my son to fly a kite.

I figure dust was here before I was born, and it will be here when I'm dead. I keep my priorities straight by asking myself, "Will this matter in a hundred years?" If the answer is no, then I don't stress over it. Sure, I clean out my refrigerator and do the laundry and run the dishwasher and clean the house. We all should do those things—at least once a year anyway. But if I have to choose between going fishing with my kids while watching the sun set on an East Texas pier or having dish soap up to my elbows, I always choose the fishing and sunset. The dishes always manage to get done. But those hours on the pier…and at the tea parties…and flying kites…will slip away and never return.

SURVIVAL SKILL

> Buy a box of 50 safety pins and place them near the washing machine. Before washing socks, pin each pair together at the top or toe. This way they never get separated from each other and folding them is a snap. This method also serves as a laundry alarm. You know it's time to fold clothes when all 50 safety pins are gone!

Imagine yourself twenty years from now, looking back.
Think about what you'll wish you had done—and do it.

Dusting

A house becomes a home when you can write
"I love you" on the furniture.
I can't tell you how many countless hours
that I have spent cleaning!
I used to spend at least eight hours every weekend making
sure things were just perfect "in case someone came over."
Then I realized one day that no one came over;
they were all out living life and having fun!
Now when people visit, I find no need to explain
the condition of my home.
They are more interested in hearing about the things
I've been doing while I was away living life and having fun.
If you haven't figured this out yet, please heed this advice:
Life is short. Enjoy it!

Dust if you must, but wouldn't it be better
to paint a picture or write a letter, bake a cake or plant a seed,
ponder the difference between want and need?
Dust if you must, but there's not much time,
with rivers to swim and mountains to climb,
music to hear and books to read, friends to cherish and life to lead.
Dust if you must, but the world's out there with the sun in your eyes,
the wind in your hair, a flutter of snow, a shower of rain.
This day will not come around again.
Dust if you must, but bear in mind,
old age will come and it's not kind.
And when you go—and go you must—you,
yourself will make more dust!

—Author unknown.

9

A Lethal Van Mama

Cutting loose the anchors, they left them in the sea
and at the same time untied
the ropes that held the rudders.
Then they hoisted the foresail to the wind and
made for the beach. But the ship struck a sandbar
and ran aground. The bow stuck fast and
would not move, and the stern was broken
to pieces by the pounding of the surf.

ACTS 27:40-41

A few years ago my husband and I bought a used van. This was my first time regularly driving a van, and I'm glad I gained experience on an old one. Driving a full-sized van is like driving a boat—especially when you've been used to an economy car.

In that van I bumped into a vehicle in the church parking lot, tangled my bumper with my housekeeper's car bumper, ripped the side trim off when I snagged it on someone else's bumper at my kid's school, and almost sideswiped my babysitter's Suburban—all on the same day. And I never did learn to park that boat straight.

After I'd bumped around town for a few years, God provided us with a nearly new van. This was one of those vehicle deals you dream of finding. A retired gentleman had purchased a brand-new, fully loaded conversion van for travel. Because his wife's health began declining, he wound up parking the van in his garage when it had less than 7,000 miles on it. He sold it to us for a fraction of the original cost. It still reeked of new vehicle odor!

By the time we drove our pristine van into our driveway, I was thanking the Lord that I'd made all my boat-driving mistakes in the old vehicle. I've been the primary driver of the new van for several years now. I still can't park completely straight, but my navigation skills have certainly improved—unless you count the bit of paint I chipped off on the Fed-Ex curb…or the trim I ripped off above the wheel…or the tiny dent I put in it at a gas pump curb. Okay, so I'm still learning. But at least I didn't run over the gas pump. Not bad for a lethal van mama!

Sometimes navigating through life is like driving a vehicle…or a boat. Some seasons flow smoothly, and there aren't even any jolts. Other times are much like my usual van-driving experience. You may be struggling to learn the ropes of a new situation and hit a few unexpected bumps along the way. You might even "tangle bumpers" with somebody else.

Then life can throw you those situations where you feel like you really have run over a gas pump, or, like Paul in the New Testament, experienced a shipwreck. The circumstances can pound you like unforgiving surf ready to tear your life to pieces. Such wrecks can come in the form of a death, divorce, career loss, or financial struggle.

Unfortunately, life isn't a *Leave It to Beaver* experience for most people. God never promised that it would be. In the real world, some wives are divorced by husbands who disappear and never pay child support for their children. That was the fate of one of my grandmothers. Other moms are widowed with a houseful of children to support from the ages of three to teenagers. That was my other grandmother's lot in life. Other mothers face their worst nightmare when the phone call comes that their child has unexpectedly died. Two of my aunts and my grandmothers have suffered this pain. Some parents have to look at their daughters and say, "I'm sorry. We just don't have the money for college. You're going to have to pay your own way through." One of those daughters was me. Other households suffer from economic fluctuations, and parents have to explain to their children why they're selling the farm, uprooting them from all their friends, and moving to the city where there are jobs. Other mothers might really want to stay home full-time but their husbands are ministers of small churches that offer low pay. So the wives' working enables them to afford insurance, to feed and clothe their children, and to save for college and retirement. I have several mom friends in ministry who work for their families' very survival.

But no matter what place you find yourself, one thing is sure: Jesus Christ is the supreme navigator through all life situations. Jesus never truly condemned people when He walked the earth, and He still doesn't. Life happens. We all live in the real world. And in the real world we're faced with circumstances not of our own choosing that we must find the strength to steer through.

So many times we think we've got to manage it all. From there, we can go into a stress-fueled tailspin. But the best thing to do is to take our hands off the wheel of our lives and allow the Lord to guide us through. Thankfully, He doesn't lecture us about how our lives should be more ideal. Instead, He places His arms around us and holds us steady.

SURVIVAL SKILL

Rubbing alcohol removes regular pen ink from clothing like magic. The alcohol dissolves the ink and leaves no trace behind.

God's perfect will isn't a one-size-fits-all,
cookie-cutter plan for every person.

10

Rest Robbers

By the seventh day God had finished the work he had been doing;
so on the seventh day he rested from all his work.

Genesis 2:2

My friend Martha Rogers has three sons. When her sons were young, she and they established a rule to help Martha keep her sanity after a full day of teaching high school. They all came home together, and after a snack, the boys were to take care of themselves for thirty minutes so Martha could relax and gather her wits. Martha's only rule: Do not kill each other. Usually the boys played games in their rooms, watched TV, or did their homework.

One afternoon Martha decided to take a quick nap. Quiet reigned supreme as the boys worked on school assignments. Toward the end of the half hour, she heard a rustling noise and thought Mike, her youngest, had sneaked into the room. Without opening an eye, Martha told Mike to go back to his brothers and wait for her to come out.

Still the rustling continued.

Now a little perturbed, Martha raised up to scold her son. On the end of the bed, contemplating her with beady brown eyes, sat a squirrel, his bushy tail arched behind him.

She screamed. The squirrel squealed and jumped from the bed. Of course the boys came running, and the little animal raced through the open door. They chased him for fifteen minutes, waving brooms and towels to get him out. He wouldn't go near the open back door. The poor critter was frightened nearly to death. Finally he found the fireplace, scooted up the chimney, and disappeared. They discovered the screen was torn at the top of the chimney and deduced the rodent had invaded the house through the hole.

A few weeks later a squirrel threw pieces of a pinecone down on Martha while she worked in a flowerbed under a tree. She figured it was the same little squirrel who wanted her out of his space as much as she'd wanted him out of hers.[1]

I have never had a squirrel invade my home via my chimney, but I did have a visitor of the winged variety trapped in my fireplace. When my son was about eleven months old and I was learning the true meaning of the word "exhausted," I heard something struggling inside the fireplace. This fireplace had a glass door that we shut once spring arrived. Along with the bumps and thuds, there was a pathetic cheeping that clued me into the fact that a fine feathered friend was trapped inside.

My little boy was doing the "toddler thing," holding onto the coffee table while he slobbered and learned to walk. I made sure he was secure, then moved toward the cheeping noise to free the bird. I bent down, looked through the dirty glass to no avail, and then opened the door.

A bright blue bird shot out of the fireplace, soared toward the ceiling, and began circling the room while furiously chirping. Brett, still gripping the coffee table's edge, looked up and followed the bird's path. In order to keep up with the blue bird, Brett's little head bobbed with the creature's every rotation. That resulted in his body swaying to the rhythm of the noisy bird's circular flight. My son, having never seen the likes, looked as if he was doing some sort of a new dance. Even in the midst of my toddler's-mom tiredness, I couldn't miss the humor.

I hurried to the back door, flung it open, and hoped the bird would notice his escape route. The poor thing was so traumatized by his plight, he kept squawking and spinning while Brett kept doing "The Blue Bird Dance." Finally the bird noticed the back door and swooped from the living room into the great outdoors. Brett went back to his slobbering as if nothing had happened. The invasion that lasted less than a minute provided me with a memory I will chuckle about the rest of my life.

Whether your kids are toddlers, elementary-school age, or teens, being a mother can make you feel like your space has been invaded, your sleep has been robbed, and you live from one crisis to another. Sometimes these might involve a squirrel on the end of the bed or a bluebird stuck in the fireplace, but more than likely, they take the form of financial situations, health issues, or an over-stuffed schedule.

Whatever the case, most moms report that they spend a lot of time tired beyond belief. I have been there. Trying to deal with two small children while writing from home has, at times, left me sleep deprived beyond all logical thought. One time my son handed me something and in response I said, "You're welcome" instead of "Thank you." My husband laughed out loud at me. I said, "Oh man, I'm so tired I'm not even thinking straight."

Simply being a mother is a full-time job. Keeping up with a household is another full-time job. Many moms also work from their homes or hold down careers. Whatever your situation, chances are high you spend a good portion of your time wishing you could have slept one or two more hours last night.

On days like this, I've found that it's helpful to emulate Martha Rogers. I've learned that lying down to rest for thirty minutes or even an hour gives me the extra boost I need to finish my day. The older I get, the more I realize that I'm less good for myself, my kids, or God when I'm so tired I cannot see straight. When I'm rested, the kids get on my nerves less, I'm more self-controlled, and I'm more capable of making sound decisions.

In the creation story, the Bible states that God rested the seventh day, after spending six days creating squirrels and birds and people and such. If God enjoyed a rest, then we should as well. Along with those occasional catnaps during the week and making sure I get a good night's rest, for me that also equates into a Sunday afternoon coma.

Feel free to carve out your own rest schedule. Your family will thank you and God will smile.

SURVIVAL SKILL

Antibiotics kill bacteria. The problem is that in killing bad bacteria, antibiotics can also kill the good bacteria living in your intestines. This often causes diarrhea. The remedy lies in eating yogurt with live cultures, or "good bacteria." When you eat yogurt, you are replacing the bacteria in your intestines that the antibiotic has killed. After every antibiotic dose, eat a few bites of yogurt. I have done this with my children since they were babies and old enough to swallow yogurt. Remember, when buying yogurt, make sure the carton says "active, live cultures."

Resting in Jesus not only involves being still before Him
but also releasing our problems to Him.

11

Through the Eyes of a Child

When I was a child, I talked like a child,
I thought like a child, I reasoned like a child.
When I became a man, I put childish ways behind me.

1 CORINTHIANS 13:11

Kids say some really funny things in their attempts to learn to talk and reason. For instance, once Brett started poking his fingers into my husband's mouth. Brett was only about three at the time and was really exploring his world. After close inspection of my husband's teeth, Brett began pressing upon Daniel's gums.

He said, "What is that pink stuff by your teeth?"

Daniel said, "That's my gums."

Brett said, "Is it strawberry?"

When Brooke was little, she came up with all sorts of interesting things. When we adopted her from Vietnam, she entered America and encountered a plethora of new sights and sounds. The first time I poured her a bowl of Raisin Bran cereal, she refused to eat it.

I said, "Yummy! Raisin Bran! Cereal. Yummy!" And showed her how to eat it.

Brooke emphatically shook her head. "No!"

I chimed in with a few more rounds of mommy encouragement, but the stubborn set of her chin never altered.

Finally she pronounced one simple word: "Bugs!"

She thought the raisins were bugs, and she refused to eat the Raisin Bran.

When Brett was three, my husband and I took him fishing in our boat. That boat had real character. A beautiful shade of faded lime green, it looked as if it dated back to the days of Noah. There we sat in our watercraft when a truly splendid emerald-colored ski boat appeared behind us. At the back of it, behind the seats, a large, flat area provided enough space for an adult to lie down in the sun.

In this boat were six to eight young women, appearing to be in their early twenties. If they had pieced together all the material from their scanty bikinis, I doubt one modest swimsuit could have been formed. All but one of the girls sat in the front of the boat, either in seats or on the edge, near the driver's seat. The other one was lying facedown on the back part of the boat.

In these positions, they cruised behind our family. Brett sharply turned his little head and began intently peering over his shoulder toward the passengers. As they trolled directly behind us, Brett turned and continued his scrutiny over his shoulder. I could almost see his mind whirling with the implications of this sight before him. I said nothing, waiting for him to voice his thoughts.

With stoic resolve, he pronounced his interpretation of the scene before him: "All those girls [a meaningful pause] are in their underwear! [Another weighty pause] And that one on the back is *dead!*"

My husband and I almost fell out of the boat laughing.

Kids really can fill our world with fresh impressions of things we see every day. And while their antics and words are often hilarious, by the time they are in their preteen years, they grow out of the baby phase and show signs of the adult waiting to emerge upon the world. Soon they're teenagers…young adults, and they start acting like it. And that's the way it should be.

That's the way we should be spiritually as well. When we live from one year to the next and never grow out of the baby phase, we stagnate spiritually. As women of God, we are called to teach our children about the world while modeling how mature Christians behave and think. A woman who is truly Christ-centered will gradually grow out of childish behavior and thought patterns such as throwing fits, criticizing, putting herself first, and petty jealousies. She'll blossom into a spiritual adult who puts God first and her family next, values the feelings of others, and applauds successes—even when they aren't her own.

SURVIVAL SKILL

If your hem is falling out of your skirt or pants and you don't have time to sew it, secure the fabric with Scotch tape or shipping tape until you have time to fix it.

A woman who seeks the Lord with her whole heart will
emulate Christ in such a way that others will say,
"If you want to know what Jesus looks like, look at her."

12

A Wet Washing Machine

Moses answered the people, "Do not be afraid.
Stand firm and you will see the
deliverance the LORD will bring you today....
The LORD will fight for you;
you need only to be still."...Then the LORD said to Moses,
"Stretch out your hand over the sea
so that the waters may flow back over
the Egyptians and their chariots and horsemen."
Moses stretched out his hand over the sea,
and at daybreak the sea went back to its place.
The Egyptians were fleeing toward it, and
the LORD swept them into the sea.

EXODUS 14:13-14,26-27

Alicia Johnson and her husband, Ronnie, had been married about five years when Ronnie was called to pastor a church in a small, East Texas town. Alicia especially liked the fact that this church had a three-bedroom parsonage since the couple had lived in various apartments while Ronnie was in graduate school. Living in apartments had also meant using laundromats. So upon moving into the parsonage, they retrieved their own washing machine from storage and installed it.

Ronnie assured Alicia that hooking up a washing machine to existing water fixtures would be no problem, even for less-than-handy people like them. She watched him attach the cold water hose to the proper faucet, the hot water hose to the other fixture, and place the drain hose into the drain pipe in the wall. After plugging the washing machine cord into the electrical outlet, he declared the hook-up complete. He suggested they try it out to make sure everything worked properly before they put a load of clothes inside. They waited as the machine tub filled, the agitator swished, and the water started out the drain hose.

That's when the problems began!

Some of the water went down fine, but suddenly the drainpipe started backing up. Soon water was going everywhere. There was a small mop bucket nearby. Ronnie grabbed it and moved the washer's hose from the stopped-up drain line to inside the bucket, which would be filled in a matter of seconds.

"Quick, get another bucket!"

Alicia ran outside. The only larger item she spotted that would hold water was an ice chest. By the time she arrived with the ice chest, the first bucket was overflowing. Ronnie handed Alicia the bucket with a splash and put the hose into the ice chest. She had plenty of time to empty the smaller bucket and get back before the ice chest was full. But there just wasn't enough time to empty it and get back before the small bucket overflowed. They managed to catch most of the water, but there was still a lot of mopping left to do after the washer had pumped off the water.

The machine then went into the rinse cycle and began filling the tub with more water. Their water-logged conversation went something like this:

"Great, now more water will be pumped out when this cycle is over."

"Quick! Unplug the machine so it will stop."

"No, just turn it off."

Looking at each other, it dawned on them that they could have simply turned off the machine earlier, and it would have quit pumping water onto the floor several bucketsful before.[1]

Sometimes our attempts to deal with our children are much like Ronnie and Alicia's topsy-turvy washing machine escapade. In our struggle to be good moms, we spend valuable time trying to fervently fix problems that really have simple answers. Those answers will very likely come if we take the time to be silent in the middle of chaos and listen to the still small voice of God.

Many times when my kids have done something that I'm tempted to overreact about or start yelling over, I say, "Okay, just a minute. Give me a second to get my composure here." Then I go into the other room, take some deep breaths, focus, pray, and calm down. More often than not, the Lord will flood my mind with insight that will sweep away the problem as effectively as the Red Sea destroyed the Egyptians. Equipped with a calm mind and a clear focus, I go back to the situation with a level head and a sensible solution. This stops me from saying something I might regret or dishing out punishment that isn't fair. It also enables me to see exactly what "button" I should push to put an end to the crisis and prevent similar issues in the future.

SURVIVAL SKILL

Old-fashioned wooden clothespins are an indispensable tool in the kitchen. I use them for all my bag clips—for chips, bread, candy, etc. They aren't fancy or cute, but they're cheap, durable, and practical. My pantry has a wire bread basket attached to the inside of the door. I clip the clothespins in rows on the wires. Placing a basket under the sink is another good option for clothespin storage.

If you listen to your kids, they'll tell you
what they're thinking and feeling and give you
plenty of hints about how you can be a better parent.
Treat them in a way that encourages openness and honesty.

13

Bald Hamsters

Train up a child in the way he should go,
and when he is old he will not turn from it.

PROVERBS 22:6

All domesticated animals have at one time been wild. Degus are wild in Chile. They also can be wild at my friend Gail Sattler's house. Degus are little rodents—picture a cross between a mouse and a squirrel. They are small, curious, adventurous, and cute and cuddly. They're also great at using the smallest opportunity to escape.

Many small rodent owners, especially owners of hamsters, live with the fear of their pets escaping. They have been known to eat holes in couches and live there. Or, if not in a couch, they are stealthy and could live loose for a long time and not be found.

One evening, during her son's absence, Gail went into his room to feed the Degus. She discovered they had eaten a hole in the corner of their plastic cage bottom and escaped. The trail led to the sewing/laundry room, where piles and more piles of stuff was stored. Sewing supplies. Laundry. Books. Toys. Luggage. Bookshelves. Boxes and bags of yarn. Half-finished projects.

Degu heaven.

Once she started digging through the piles, Gail could hear the little critters scampering for better hiding spots. But so could the dogs!

Degus are rodents, but they're still pets. Not much is scarier than the worry of one pet killing another. What parent wants to tell their children that mommy's pet ate their pet?

The race was on.

With the dogs at one end of the room and Gail on the other, clothing flew in the air. Balls of yarn were launched. Boxes skidded. Items Gail hadn't seen for years appeared out of nowhere. When a dog started nosing frantically in one spot, Gail was right behind, then in front, risking teeth and life and limb.

One Degu was located and herded into a hamster ball for return into its safe cage.

The other ran into what it thought was a tube, but it was a cone of serger-style thread. The degu managed to wedge himself into that cone. Gail made it to the cone a split second before the dog and carried the wedged rodent—bottom high in the air—across the room. The dog bounced along beside her before she popped the degu back into its cage.[1]

When I was a kid, degus weren't around. But my family did have pet gerbils. Once my mother was trying to clean the gerbil's cage and it escaped. Instead of heading into the wide beyond, the rodent scurried up my mother's arm. As much as she grabbed for him, she missed him every time. Soon the critter reached her shoulder.

In an attempt to escape my mom's clutches, it scurried near her hairline and burrowed under the neck of her dress. The gerbil's little claws scratched against my mom's skin as he maneuvered himself to that position in the middle of her back where she couldn't reach.

By this point, my mother was on the verge of panicking. She was at our apartment alone and couldn't grab the gerbil. She was also overcome with her fear of mice, and this gerbil felt more like a mouse than a pet. Tempted to erupt into a screaming fit, she kept her cool and finally managed to extract the rodent from beneath her dress.

That same gerbil got loose in our apartment. It nearly went wild before we were able to capture him. We would be watching TV and realize we were being watched. "There he is!" one of us would shout. And the whole family would lunge toward the gerbil.

We did finally manage to keep the gerbil in his cage, and he went with us when we moved to Arkansas. But we hadn't been there long when our new cat ate him—just gobbled him up like a delicacy.

Considering my gerbil history and Gail's degus experience, when my kids begged for a hamster, I was a bit dubious. I could just see myself waking in the middle of the night with a hamster on my face, staring me eye-to-eye. Not as flamboyant as waking to a boa constrictor staring me eye-to-eye, but still not a scenario I wanted to endure. I also imagined myself scrounging through the laundry room in search of an escapee. Furthermore, we own five cats, and three spend a significant amount of time indoors. I had flashbacks to the tragic day when my cat ate my gerbil.

After arguing and cajoling and begging, my kids convinced me I should allow them to purchase a couple of teddy bear hamsters. We struck a deal. They would use their saved money to buy everything. I also made sure they understood they would be responsible for the rodents' upkeep. I explained they would have to feed them, water them, and change the wood shavings in the bottom of the cage.

"Those shavings cost $3 for a large bag," I explained. "And you'll be responsible for paying for the food and the shavings."

My daughter, Brooke, looked up and exclaimed, "You mean every time you shave the hamsters we have to pay you $3?"

At that point, our whole household went into outlandish hysterics. I laughed so hard I flopped on the couch, clutched my midsection, and cried. My son guffawed. My husband, in the laundry room ironing his clothes, started laughing out loud. As I tried to answer my genuinely confused daughter, all I could envision was holding a bald hamster in one hand and a used disposable razor in the other.

Finally I explained to Brooke that we wouldn't be shaving the hamsters, but the wood pieces in the bottom of the cage were called wood shavings. I further detailed that a bag of wood shavings cost $3, but would last quite a while. And I expected her to be financially responsible for the upkeep of her hamsters. At last she understood.

In an attempt to teach my children about money, I have given them an allowance since they were preschoolers. When they were younger, I made them save their allowance until they hit $20. Now that they're older, they save until they hit $30. When they arrive at the right amount, we have what we call "break out." That means they get to retrieve their money from their banks. Then they give 10 percent to the church. I have them save another 10 percent. With the money that's left, they can purchase something useful, such as an educational toy, clothing, or a souvenir from one of our trips. At the release of this book, they'll be opening savings accounts to start saving for their first cars and college.

Earned allowances makes your kids appreciate money and give them a clue about the value of a dollar. It also gives them the initiative to do their chores. As I am working on this book, my nearly nine-year-old daughter has come into the room with a bottle of glass cleaner and a can of furniture polish. She's taking the initiative in cleaning the windows and dusting the furniture because she's decided she wants a Game Boy, and she knows she'll get paid for cleaning.

Making children financially responsible also gives parents an effective vehicle for enforcing discipline. For instance, if you tell a child not to play with the new camera, you can add, "And if you do and you break it, you will pay to have it fixed." My kids know I will follow through—even if it costs a hundred bucks—so they don't risk their money for an act of disobedience. Now, if the broken camera does not involve an act of disobedience but a pure-hearted mistake, I give my children ample grace and don't make them pay to have it fixed. Furthermore, making a four-year-old earn enough money to feed a horse or an eight-year-old pay a high veterinary bill is illogical.

I want my children to get a taste of financially supporting themselves now so that when they are grown they won't expect me to financially support them. So many times parents complain about their grown children financially depending on them. But what they don't realize is that the grown children are usually continuing a pattern that was engrained during childhood. As parents, we are called to prepare our children for the real world, for real problems, and for the potential of financial solvency.

So when my kids started asking for hamsters, I told them I would expect them to be financially responsible for the pets. They readily agreed and asked if they could use the money they had saved to purchase the creatures. I agreed that these sorts of special occasions were the reason they saved money.

Now our family is the proud new owner of two hamsters. Last night was our first escape incident. One of those little guys got out of its ball—a free-rolling plastic device that allows the hamsters access to the whole house while they remain captive. Last night we found a ball with the lid off. The hamster was nowhere to be found. Finally my son spotted one of our cats fearfully watching the hamster. Unlike my childhood cat, that feline is *afraid* of our hamsters.

SURVIVAL SKILL

Many times when my kids are begging me for something, I tell them they're free to buy it with their own money if they like. About three-fourths of the time, this stops the begging and ends their desire. When they know *their* money is on the line, it can change everything.

Often those annoying kid things,
such as pet rodents,
can create the most lasting and humorous
family memories.

14

The Family Purse

"Many women do noble things, but you surpass them all."
Charm is deceptive, and beauty is fleeting; but a woman who
fears the LORD is to be praised.

PROVERBS 31:29-30

Businessmen have it so good! Somebody with a lot of insight invented a great purse for men and called it a briefcase. I've wanted a purse like that for years—with all the pockets and slots and holders. That way everything has its place, and there's no chance of the mass confusion so many women's purses lend themselves to. But they don't make a briefcase in the size I need. Most briefcases are proportionately created to fit a hulking man, not an average-sized woman. For years I've looked for a case that is about half the size of a normal briefcase but a little thicker. I had almost despaired of ever finding what I needed until a recent trip to the office supply store.

There, nestled on the shelf, I found it! A case exactly the size I had been searching for. To top it off, someone had designed it in silver, so it looked less like a traditional briefcase. I was elated! I bought my new "purse," took it home, and showed it to my best friend—my husband.

Daniel said, "Oh! That's so pretty! But I don't think you'll be able to get all your stuff in that case. It looks kind of small."

"But you don't know who you're dealing with!" I said. "I can make this work. I really can! It's exactly what I've been looking for."

Daniel shook his head and smirked (of all the nerve!) as I flopped open my new purse on the dining room table and began to fill it with my stuff. He followed that smirk with a chuckle and leaned against the breakfast bar.

"I really think that's a great case," he said with an indulgent smile, "and I could use it in my locksmith business." Daniel crossed his arms. "I've got some papers I've been needing a case just like that for."

I did something really spiritual—I narrowed my eyes and said, "Not on your life, Buddy! You aren't going to get my purse!"

He laughed outright. "Yes, I will," he claimed. "There's no way you're going to fit all the junk from your purse in there. And when you accept defeat, I'll be glad to accept the case."

By this time, I was more determined than ever to make the new purse work. I was in the throes of arranging and rearranging all my electronics and other important stuff (that my best friend had the audacity to call junk). After a particularly exasperating round of fighting to shut the case against the bulge within, I looked back at Daniel and declared with a teasing grin, "I'm not going to give you this case. If I can't get it to work, I'm taking it back to the office store. If you want it, you'll have to go buy it yourself!"

"Ooooo," he taunted, "you're a *mean*-spirited woman!"

We both enjoyed an abundance of laughter.

"Just wait," I vowed, "I will make this case work. It's exactly… what…I…need," I finished through gritted teeth as I attempted to close it once more.

By the next morning, I realized my dreams of the silver case becoming my new purse would not be fulfilled. With the demeanor of a gracious warrior, I removed my possessions from the case and extended it to my husband.

"Here," I said, "you were right. I hope you enjoy my new purse."

Daniel chuckled and took my purse without so much as an apology or a sympathetic pat on the back. The last time I saw it was in his locksmith van, full of his stuff. I promise, the briefcase stuck out its tongue and said, "Naa na-na-na-na!" like a spoiled child.

Now, I carry a purse that looks like a small piece of luggage, similar to a doctor's bag. It opens up almost like an accordion when all the compartments are unzipped. This purse has a place for a cell phone, checkbook, and credit cards with all sorts of added compartments inside and outside. It works like a portable file folder and is great for keeping bills and receipts separate from personal items like lipstick and keys.

It's also great when traveling with my family. When we're on the road, we fondly dub my purse "the family purse" or "THE PURSE." Before we get a hundred miles from home, it seems like every family member has something in that purse. Brooke's chapstick. Brett's Game Boy game. My husband's fingernail clippers. Our ministry's money. Of course, the thirty-three lipsticks belong to me. The thing gets so heavy Daniel usually winds up carrying it. If you ever see a linebacker sort hauling a purse through an airport with a glazed-eyed woman beside him, then you've seen us!

Interestingly enough, I can usually keep up with everything that's in that purse. Oh, occasionally I might lose something unimportant, like my keys. But for the most part I can stick my fingers into that great black hole and come up with what I'm searching for.

But isn't that the way many moms are? Whether it's our purses or our laps, we can be the source of comfort for our families.

Any time I'm tempted to get exasperated about my kids yelling, "Mom, I need…" I try to remind myself that they *really do* need. They need me. They need me to be there. They need me to comfort, to care, to kiss their wounds. They know I can reach into my purse or my heart or my pantry and pull out exactly the right thing to make it all better. Whether that's a tissue, a hug, or a bowl of chicken soup, I am needed. I am loved.

SURVIVAL SKILL

Any time you get gum stuck in hair or on clothing or furniture, place a piece of ice on the gum until it hardens. Then the gum easily peels away.

Moms are the glue that holds the family together.

Strange Things Women Have Found in Their Purses

Money

Husband's tools

Bra

Plate from Pizza Hut

Dead fish in bag

Dirty jock strap

Nest of earwigs

Dirty diaper

Vomit

Spilled bottle of pancake syrup

Chicken nugget—hardened
   with age

Rubber cockroach

Night crawler

Angler worm

Drooled-on dog biscuit

Tomato seeds

Husband

Catnip mouse

Dried chunks of mud

Melted chocolate

Purple squishy dinosaur

Melted caramel

Used paint stick

Underwear

Rubber hairy spider

Lemon salt water taffy

Rubber snake

Moldy pizza

Last night's happy meal

Onion peels

Chewed gum

Iced tea

Candy wrappers

Ants

False teeth

Round tuit

Deodorant

Buckeye and acorn

Jewish cookbook

Walnut

Panty hose

Rocks

Dirty spoon

Two Doritoes

Tire pressure gauge

Mace

Screwdriver

Turkey call

Month-old sandwich

Orange that had molded and
   sprouted "legs"

Tucks

Pliers

Tape measure

Dried up flower

Dried cat food

Vampire teeth

CPR microshield

Matchbox cars

Statue of Yoda

Salt and pepper shakers

Plastic eyeball

Banana peel

Dead batteries

Old Cheerios

Whistle

Crushed crackers

Melted butter

Dog drool

15

Roaming the Roof and Loving It!

*Deborah, a prophetess, the wife of Lappidoth, was leading Israel
at that time. She held court under the Palm of Deborah between
Ramah and Bethel in the hill country of Ephraim, and the Israelites
came to her to have their disputes decided.*

JUDGES 4:4-5

Dogs are as unique as their owners, but some dogs are more unique than others. When Gail Sattler got her new puppy, a Standard Schnauzer, she had no idea how true this was going to be. She'd had the puppy home for barely over a week when she heard a knock on the door. It was her neighbor Dave, with a question.

"Do you know your dog is on the roof of your house?" he asked.

Gail looked toward her roof. The house was constructed with a ground level entry that lead to the basement. The main living level was the second story. From the living room bay window, there was a section of roof that acted as an overhang. Joining the overhang, another angled section was the peak of the built-in garage. At this point, the puppy was able to access the roof.

And yes, he was on the roof and having the time of his life.

Gail ran up the stairs and opened a window as fast as she could. Eight-week-old puppies aren't exactly known for obedience. Soon, with a bit of convincing and a lot of bribery, the puppy was back inside. Gail thought the problem was solved until the next day when the same thing happened. Along with the next day, and the day after that.

Soon having a dog on the roof became expected, even normal. Ina spent most of her summer days on the roof. Very sure-footed, she freely pranced back and forth. Her favorite spot was the peak of the garage roof, where she sat like a gargoyle, watching the neighborhood happenings. This greatly amused the neighbors, but it didn't end there. To Gail's constant embarrassment, strangers halted on the sidewalks watching Ina as she ogled them right back. Motorists stopped their cars in the middle of the quiet residential street to stare at the roof dog. People stopped and pointed. A few even came to the door to ask if Gail knew her dog was on the roof. When they approached the door, they had to walk under the roof/overhang. They were met with a ferocious display of growling and beautiful white teeth from above. Ina wasn't an asset for most visitors, but she was an effective deterrent for pesky door-to-door salespeople.

When needing to give directions to other parents so they could drop their children off to play with Gail's children, no one needed many details. They all said the same thing, even people who lived miles away. "I know how to get to your house. You're the one with the dog on the roof!"

However, it was not enough of a deterrent for the SPCA. Once the SPCA staff member was convinced that the dog was safe, enjoyed her time on the roof, and had free and easy access on and off, he left, but only after making sure the dog was properly licensed.[1]

Gail's dog made her home different from any others in the city. What makes you and your home unique? Do you willingly celebrate that uniqueness…or do you spend most of your time trying to change your home or make it into something it's not? And what about you? Do you celebrate your individuality?

Early in my motherhood I spent a lot of time trying to fit the "June Cleaver" mold. The mother of Beaver Cleaver, June was the American classic TV model for the ultimate homemaker, mom, and wife. I read plenty of books and articles on being a good wife and mother and tried to do what all the experts said I was supposed to do. One day I finally realized that for me I was trying to fit a square peg into a round hole. Like Gail's dog, I just don't fit anybody's mold.

Once I realized this, I broke away from what everybody said I was supposed to be and started seeking the Lord about what He wanted me to be. God has given me a talent to write and speak and sing, and I found out He wanted me to use these gifts to His glory. This realization brought a divine balance to my life. While I am a ministry mom, my efforts are home-based, so I set my own schedule. I am free to be there for my kids for field trips, recitals, and birthdays. We usually travel as a family to my speaking engagements. My husband serves as ministry manager and my partner in song. My children participate in my ministry by helping at my book table, singing with my husband and me, and perhaps telling jokes or stories from the stage at ministry events. My kids have even watched from the sidelines as I was interviewed for a TV show. We've been privileged to see more of the U.S. than most people see in their lifetimes—Mt. Rushmore, the Badlands, the Grand Canyon, the Appalachians, the Rockies, the Pacific Ocean, and the Atlantic Ocean.

No, I don't fit the June Cleaver mold. But neither did the Old Testament prophetess Deborah. I wonder how much criticism she got during her tenure as Israel's top ranking official? I wonder how many people tried to put her into a mold. Deborah broke out of the box. She did what God told her to do.

What about you? What works best for you and your family? God may have already shown you it's His will for you to be a full-time homemaker and mom who homeschools. The Lord may have directed you and your husband to run a home-based business together.

Maybe you live near a wonderful public school where you teach and keep the same schedule as your kids do. Or you may be a single mom who is thrilled that you had the foresight to get a solid education because you now hold a position that is supporting your family. Praise God for courageous mothers!

Then again, you may be like me and Gail's dog, out running around on the roof, so to speak, while everyone else looks on and shakes their heads.

God's perfect will is not the same for every woman, man, and child. He's created each of us as individuals. Each of us has different life circumstances that God has allowed to bring us to the positions where we are. None of us needs to be poured into a mold. Have the courage to encounter the Lord and find out what *His* master plan is for your life, your home, and your children.

SURVIVAL SKILL

Leftover french fries or other fried foods get soggy after refrigeration. Baking them at 425 degrees for 5 to 10 minutes restores their crispness and makes them edible.

Every child is different. Tailor your discipline
and parenting style to fit the child.

16

Sprayed!

But thanks be to God, who always leads us in
triumphal procession in Christ and through us spreads everywhere
the fragrance of the knowledge of him.

2 CORINTHIANS 2:14

Kim Sawyer rubbed her protruding abdomen and spoke to her unborn child, as she often did as the due date neared. "Hey, Baby, mama's pooped, but your nursery is almost ready for you."

Late afternoon sun slanted through the kitchen window, and Kim headed for the back porch to soak up a few of those waning rays. She settled onto the second-to-the-bottom porch riser, stretched out her legs, and let her head drop back. Only a few more days and the baby would be here. She'd be holding it in her arms instead of carrying it inside. She was both excited and frightened at the prospect. She'd never been a mama before and sensed big changes were in store.

Something bumped the back of Kim's shins, and she looked down to see a black-and-white nose poking between the bottom two porch risers. "Hello, Button," she said. A family of cats had adopted them—a mother and six half-grown kittens. Her favorite by far was Button, a female with a sociable personality. She stuck her hand between the risers to scratch between the cat's ears.

Kim had enjoyed watching this mama cat care for her babies. The cat tolerated their playful attacks and gave them baths, holding them down with one paw. Mother instincts were evident in the cat's protectiveness toward her offspring. Kim prayed her own mother instincts would kick in. She so wanted to be a good mom.

As she continued to stroke Button's ears, Kim realized the fur felt funny. Prickly. Almost sticky. With a frown, she said, "Button, I think you need a bath. What have you gotten into?" Taking a grip on the scruff of the cat's neck, Kim tugged her from beneath the porch. To her shock she was not holding a cat, but a small skunk!

Kim released a startled squawk and let go. She was inside the kitchen, leaning against the door, almost before she knew she was moving. She watched through the window as the skunk stood at the base of the steps, looking around as if confused. It rubbed its head against the corner of the bottom step, and then ambled around the house and disappeared.

Kim's breath wooshed out, and her heart finally settled into a normal rhythm. *Have I really just stroked a skunk?* she thought. *Why didn't it spray me?* Kim finally decided it must have liked the scratching. She managed to laugh a little.

Rubbing her stomach, she informed her baby, "Oh, sweetheart, does mama have a story to tell you someday!"[1]

My family and I weren't as fortunate as Kim Sawyer. Memorial Day weekend 2002 was indeed memorable for us. It all started on Thursday night when a faint, foul odor erupted into a horrific, invisible cloud that burned our eyes and made us gag. I thought my little girl was going to throw up. You see, a skunk decided that our house was a prime target for its complimentary "air freshener." And it didn't just spray us once—it sprayed numerous times along the back of our house. We knew we were a multiple-target family because the scent came in waves. About the time the odious odor would subside, we would suddenly be accosted by another wave.

I've smelled skunk off and on my whole life, but this was the most direct hit I've ever experienced. I assure you: When you smell a skunk along the highway, that's merely a faint whiff compared to what we experienced. What invaded our nostrils that Thursday night smelled like badly burned rubber, musk perfume, nasty onions, and *skunk!* To say it was *awful* is an understatement. Nevertheless, my broad-shouldered warrior of a husband went out with a flashlight and walked around the house. I wondered what he would do with the creature if he came upon it. Fortunately, he didn't find it.

The shocking thing is that while we live in a small town, we're still in town. I thought there was some kind of an unstated wildlife law against skunks coming into town. Our neighbor had called the dog-catcher on a skunk a few weeks before. I guess we could have called the dogcatcher as well. The way the skunk population seems to be increasing in our town, if I were the dogcatcher I would probably suddenly feel "called" to pursue another career.

We finally settled down for a good night's sleep and hoped the next morning would prove less smelly. Well, it didn't! And guess what—my children had each asked a friend over to spend the night. So my kids and their friends awoke Friday morning smelling a little less than pleasant. When we took the friends home, their mothers both commented that they reeked. My son's friend's mom reported that even her child's shoes smelled like skunk!

We spent a couple of days with all the windows open in our home and the fans blowing full-time. My husband and I put our nicest clothes in our van in hopes that they hadn't absorbed the odor. My daughter's friend's mother said that I might want to check into using the 99-cent cleaners for our clothes. I responded, "Yeah, but do they do skunk?" I could just see myself calling all the cleaners in the area asking, "Do you do skunk?"

For a while when I left the house, I couldn't figure out what about me smelled so bad. Then I realized it was my purse! The inside smelled as if it had been a direct target. Even my lipstick cases smelled like skunk.

My pastor's wife, Joy, used one of our hairbrushes to brush her daughter's hair when her daughter visited us Sunday. The next time I saw Joy, she reported that her hand smelled like skunk after using the brush!

Saturday night I called my former secretary, Kim Owens. I said, "The inventory for my on-line bookstore is here in my home office. Do you think all these thousands of dollars worth of books smell like skunk?"

Kim, being the supportive sort, screamed with laughter.

I said, "This is not funny! What am I going to do? When people place their orders on the Internet, I can't ship books that smell like skunk. I guess if somebody from Europe orders books, they'll get a dose of Texas skunk right along with their books!"

Kim just screamed some more, and her hysterical laughter exploded over the line. I imagined by this point she was red-faced and near the point of unconsciousness.

"Look," I said, wondering if she was *ever* going to get a grip, "do you have a clothesline anywhere? Do you think we could pin some fabric softener sheets between the pages and hang the books on a clothesline?"

More laughter. A lot of help *she* was!

Fortunately my books weren't affected, and I'm so glad. Equally miraculous, our good clothes didn't pick up the odor either. So the 99-cent cleaners were spared! There for a few days every time I saw people I knew, I'd ask, "Do I smell like skunk?" They would sniff in my general direction and say no. What a relief!

A month after our skunk fiasco we didn't smell the odor much as long as we stayed home. But when we left and came back, we encountered that atrocious odor again.

When my "supportive" secretary came to work shortly after the skunk baptismal, she nearly swooned and said, "I can't work in these conditions."

I said, "Oh, don't worry about it! You'll get used to it soon, and then you won't even smell it." Sure enough, she became indoctrinated to the aroma of wildlife and stopped noticing the fragrance after a while.

As time wore on, the odor diminished until we could mask the essence of skunk with scented candles. And that's a good thing because this "visitation" was enough to make us all consider nose amputations!

You know, the atmosphere of our homes can be a lot like that skunk odor. If we "spray" our families with complaining, criticism, and bad attitudes, we will create a horrible family odor that can be "smelled" by the soul. If families live in this odor for years, they eventually get to the point of being unable to "spiritually smell" the odor. When visitors come in who aren't used to the odor, they can smell it. But we can't because it has become a way of life.

If you've fallen into some negative habits lately, why not allow the

Lord to give you a spiritual bath and give you the strength to break any odoriferous habits. After all, as moms we should be spreading "everywhere the fragrance of the knowledge of him."

SURVIVAL SKILL

When I mop, I never return my dirty mop to the mop bucket. Instead, after I mop each section of the floor, I rinse the mop out in the sink and get rid of all the soil I've accumulated that round. Then I dip the freshly rinsed mop into the mop water, squeeze it out, and tackle a new section of the floor. This way, I don't keep putting new dirt into my mop water and redistributing it on my floors.

It's not what you gather, but what you scatter that
tells what kind of life you have lived.

—ANONYMOUS

17

Buddha Ghost!

*For you have been my hope, O Sovereign L*ORD*,*
my confidence since my youth.
From birth I have relied on you;
you brought me forth from my mother's womb.
I will ever praise you.

PSALM 71:5-6

In 1996 my husband and I traveled to South Vietnam to adopt our daughter, Brooke. The journey took us to Ho Chi Minh City, formerly known as Saigon. This was our first international flight, and we were both somewhat concerned about safety issues. Once we arrived in Saigon, crawled into the back of a taxi, and merged into the wild, third-world traffic, we soon realized we'd been concerned about the wrong thing. International flying was a breeze compared to the lack of traffic laws and wild drivers teeming the streets.

Within two weeks, we'd gone through all the procedures to adopt our daughter except making the trip through the American Embassy in Bangkok, Thailand. Because my husband had to go back home to his job and for our son, who was staying with friends, we decided that I would stay in Vietnam for the final leg of the journey. Days after Daniel flew back to Texas, I joined the other adoptive parents in flying to Bangkok. Bangkok reminds me a lot of Dallas, TX, except it's bigger.

Furthermore, the culture is blatantly Buddhist. As tourists, we visited a Buddhist temple and saw the bald priests in their activities as well as several huge, gold-laden Buddha statues. One night after my newly adopted daughter had gone to sleep, I noticed that the Gideons had placed Bibles in the rooms. The presence of the Bible warmed my heart. But soon I also noticed the *Book of Buddha.*

As a student of literature, I'm always curious about other religious writings. From a strictly scholarly viewpoint, I picked up the *Book of Buddha* and began reading. Soon I grew tired and laid the opened book on the nightstand. Yawning, I prepared for bed, turned out the light, and crawled under the covers. I reached across the king-sized bed and patted my sleeping daughter. She didn't even stir.

I'd barely gotten comfortable when the wind started howling against the high-rise hotel. A rumble of thunder ushered in sheets of rain that crashed against the windows. Bolts of lightning crackled close. I jumped. The blinding flash and resulting booms left me rigid. I looked to the other side of the bed and was thankful my daughter was fast asleep.

I recalled many nights as a child when such storms would assault the Arkansas hills. The next morning we'd often receive reports of tornadoes that skipped through the night. I began to search my memory for anything I might have read about weather in Bangkok.

Do they have tornadoes here? I wondered and envisioned a photo I'd seen of a tornado beside an American skyscraper. The lean funnel tugged at the high-rise building while its tail curled toward the side of the structure.

I hunkered under the clean-smelling covers and prayed. Soon the storm subsided, and my nerves gradually calmed.

I was within a breath of complete relaxation when the lights in my room clicked on. My eyes popped open. I clutched the covers. My nerves escalated into a state of frenzy all over again. My first thought was that someone had somehow sneaked into my room. When I convinced myself I'd have heard the door open and close, I accepted that my daughter and I were alone. This led me to the next sequence of unstable logic.

Perhaps the lights had come on as a result of spirit activity! In a flash I relived all sorts of movies and stories I'd read about demons or ghosts. Granted, I don't believe in ghosts. But when you're in a foreign hotel room, even the most rational mind will conjure all sorts of scenarios. At this point, the worries about a tornado seemed like child's play.

Eyes wide, I barely breathed. My gaze darted from one section of the room to the other. I listened. Intensely listened. I heard nothing. Finally, I conjured the courage to scoot up in bed. As I did, the *Book of Buddha* caught my eye. There it lay open.

Oh my word! I thought as a rash of chills covered my body. *I've invited some Buddha ghost in here!*

I snatched up that *Book of Buddha,* slammed it closed, and rammed it into the nightstand's bottom drawer. The drawer had barely clapped shut when I began to get a grip on my crazed mind.

There has got to be some logical explanation for this, I thought as I swung my feet to the floor. *This is ridiculous for me to be acting this way. I'm a level-headed, grown woman.*

After another quick glance toward my serene daughter, I began to pray for the Lord's presence and strength. I also threw in an extra prayer for protection against any dark forces—just in case I really wasn't overreacting. Soon I'd investigated the bathroom and found it empty and void of any floating objects or weird moaning noises. A perusal of the door confirmed that the room was still tightly locked. I examined the light switch. Oddly, it had not been flipped, which led me to begin considering electrical issues.

The next morning at breakfast, I shared my story with another adoptive couple. We decided there must be some kind of timer set on the lights. Sure enough, when I consulted the hotel clerk, she affirmed that this was a possibility. She arranged for a maintenance man to arrive in my room. In broken English he explained that some of the rooms did have the option of scheduling the lights to come on. When the lights came on, the guest would awaken. This served as an alarm. After a few minutes, he'd deactivated the light alarm system and left my room.

As I sat in the hotel room with my daughter in my lap, I wilted with relief. I also felt goofy. But I gave myself some grace. After all, the weeks preceding the "Buddha ghost" escapade had been some of the most stressful of my entire life. Flying all the way to Asia had been exhausting. Leaving my son with friends while we traveled had twisted my mother's heart. Trying to adjust to a new daughter who was not acclimating well was taxing—and we'd only just begun that process.

Nevertheless, I pulled her close, hugged her thin, twenty-one-month-old body, and buried my nose in her black-satin hair. She smelled like baby shampoo and love. And I knew one day I'd be able to tell her that her mother flew halfway around the globe just to get her…that I picked her out of all the little girls in the world…that I'd even braved a Buddha ghost just for her. I envisioned the days when we'd hold hands and go shopping together or maybe even get our nails done together. I also knew I'd have the honor of telling her about the Lord and how I'd relied on Him since my youth…how I relied on Him during the trip to adopt her, including the scary storm and the lights with minds of their own.

Now, over seven years later, those days are here. Brooke is now nine. We shop together, get our nails done together, and laugh together. She recently wrote me a love note that said, "Thank you for coming to get me." She has accepted Christ as her Savior and is saying she wants to go back to Vietnam as a doctor missionary.

Even in that haunted room in Bangkok, I had the deep sense that I was "borrowing" Brooke, to train her to love the Lord…to praise the Lord so that one day she might go back to Vietnam. Who knows what the future holds for my Vietnamese princess. I will leave the outcome in God's hands and be forever grateful He called me to be part of His plan to raise this precious girl.

God has a plan for each and every child. Whether we adopt our children or give birth, we as godly mothers are called to help support that plan—not to hinder it with our own agenda. Have you asked the Lord to show you how you can best facilitate His plan for your children?

SURVIVAL SKILL

If you are of light complexion, you can use baby powder as a loose cosmetic powder to set your foundation. You can also mix baby powder with any loose cosmetic powder to tone down the color if it is too dark for your skin tone.

Read about Hannah,
one of the bravest mothers in the Bible.
She dedicated her son to the Lord,
and then left him in the care of Eli, the
priest, who raised him in the temple.
Samuel became one of Israel's judges
and anointed Saul as the first king of Israel.

18

"Two Words, Mama..."

Whatever is true, whatever is noble, whatever is right,
whatever is pure, whatever is lovely, whatever is admirable—
if anything is excellent or praiseworthy—think about such things.

PHILIPPIANS 4:8

A while ago I was so impressed with my son because of the godly character I was seeing him manifest. At the age of ten, he was showing significant signs of growing into a young man who thought of the well-being of others above his own. Not only was he making choices to do what was right, but he was also defending children who'd been wronged. He'd exhibited many of these traits at church one day when he defended a small child against a bully, and I decided to profusely praise him for his efforts.

He was lying on the bed watching television. I bent down to him, and at eye level I said, "Brett, I'm thrilled you are my son. And I'm really impressed with the young man I see emerging within you. You are really showing signs of strong character. I'm so honored to be your mother."

I waited, looked directly into Brett's face, fully expecting him to shine with pleasure while saying something profound like, "My dearest and most blessed mother. You have no idea how much your kind words have meant to me this glorious and mighty day. I will cherish your praise until I am old and gray. You, above all women, are impacting my life, and I have the examples of you and my most admirable father to thank for the character you see shining forth in me."

But instead of the wondrous spiel I so longed to hear, Brett simply said, "Two words, Mama."

I lovingly said, "What, Brett?" and breathlessly anticipated his accolades.

But Brett hadn't read my mental script. He had insights of his own. *"Breath mint!"* he bluntly replied, yet his eyes revealed a hint of that preadolescent I-loved-that-Mom-but-I've-got-to-act-like-I-didn't.

That was good enough for me. I laughed, straightened, and thought, *Well, so much for that!*

Regardless of my need for a breath mint, regardless of Brett's preteen quip, I still believe my son will carry my words with him for life. I affirmed the growth I've seen in him. The more I applaud his good traits, the more of those traits he'll act out.

I have committed to a lifetime of regularly building up my children with praise. The more positively we speak to children, the more positively they'll behave. Children often give back to us what we put into them. According to Judy Cornelia Pearson and Paul Edward Nelson, in their book *Understanding and Sharing*, this is called self-fulfilling prophecy.[1] Children will live out what you tell them they are. If you repeatedly criticize children, they will act more negatively. They will also speak more negatively to you. If you tell children they are valuable and dwell on the good they have done, they will repeat the good. They will also speak more positively to you—unless, of course, you have bad breath.

So many times families fall into negative behavioral patterns that are passed from one generation to the next. Think back to your own childhood. Were your parents committed to praising you, or did they spend more time criticizing you? Now contemplate your relationship with your children. You might be surprised how much that relationship reflects the one you had with your own parents. If your relationship with your parents was healthy and positive, then you are probably pleased at this point. If your relationship with your parents had room for improvement, you may be troubled to see the same patterns in your relationships with your own children.

If there is room for growth, there is no better time to start the process than now. Place a rubber band on your wrist. If you find yourself criticizing your children, pull the rubber band tight and release it against your wrist. That snap and sting will remind you to stop the pattern and begin a new one. After popping yourself with the rubber band, pray that God will give you the strength to live out Philippians 4:8. Then commit to saying something positive about your child.

None of this is a replacement for balanced correction or needed discipline. Even the best child must have correction and a parent who is firm and honest about misdeeds. However, I have found that regularly praising my children gives them the fuel to produce more good behavior than bad.

SURVIVAL SKILL

Always use distilled water in steam irons. Tap water is full of impurities. The tap water impurities settle in the iron's water well and collect. Eventually the steam iron will begin to "spit" dingy water spots on your clothing.

Any time I'm tempted to gripe about one of my children's messes around the house, I remind myself that I've either got messes as bad as theirs or at some time in my life I've made messes as bad as theirs.

19

Long-Tailed Visitors

Catch for us the foxes, the little foxes
that ruin the vineyard.

SONG OF SONGS 2:15

When I was ten, my father was the pastor of a small church in the hills of Arkansas. The parsonage we called home was an old house that was well ventilated. Whatever the temperature was outside, that was the temperature inside—summer and winter.

Aside from a small bathroom heater, the only source of heat in the house was the large rock fireplace in the living room. On one side of the living room, we'd close the bedroom door. On the other side, we hung up a blanket in the wide walkway between the living room and dining room. What heat didn't escape up the chimney would be captured in the living room. At least one room in the house was warm all the time! Since some of the panes in my and my sister's bedroom had been broken, the cold winter breezes passed through our bedroom. We stayed warm in our beds with an electric blanket and piles of covers.

In the summer, we raised the windows and suffered through the heat with box fans. I remember going to sleep to the melodies of crickets, hoot owls, and whippoorwills. The smells of honeysuckle and pines and oaks danced through our dreams. Just about the time you thought a hot humid night couldn't get any more "special," a mosquito would buzz through and spend the next few hours dive bombing our ears.

But mosquitoes weren't the only wildlife we encountered. During one of our ventilated summers, my mother opened the pantry and spotted what she thought was a large rat. She started screaming bloody murder about the rat in the pantry. My father raced into the kitchen with my sister and me close behind.

"There's a huge rat in there!" she bellowed.

My father stepped into the pantry to observe a gray creature with a long tail and a pointy nose staring back at him. "That's not a rat," he said. "It's a possum!"

"A possum!" my mother yelped. "How did a possum get in our pantry?"

"I have no idea," my father replied. Not knowing what else to do, my dad stepped into the pantry, grabbed the possum by his tail and backed into the kitchen. The possum, as disillusioned with us as we were with him, wrapped his tail around my dad's fingers, wilted, and hung in the air as limp as a used up dish towel. My sister and I followed my parents into the backyard. My father dropped the possum on the grass. The terrified creature played dead.

"He's playing possum," my father explained. "If they're scared, they play dead because they want whatever is bothering them to leave them alone. That's why we say if somebody's pretending to be asleep, they're 'playing possum.'"

My sister and I had heard that cliché our whole lives, but now we were getting a real life example of it.

Finally our family decided to leave the poor critter alone. We all went back into the house so the possum could get up and amble back to the woods. At that point, we thought we'd seen the last of our pointy-faced friend.

We were wrong.

A few days later my mother placed a chicken on the counter to thaw for our dinner that evening. When she went back into the kitchen to begin dinner preparations, her first thought was to cut up the chicken for frying. She glanced toward the area of the counter where she'd left the bird only to see nothing. There was no sign of that chicken, although she specifically recalled exactly where she'd left it.

Soon she noticed something wedged between the refrigerator and the end of the cabinet. On closer inspection, she realized the "some-thing" was her chicken. Gritting her teeth, she dislodged the chicken from between the cabinet and the fridge and saw that the tip of the poor thing's tail bone had been chewed off.

Her mind traveled back to the possum scenario from a few days before, and she wondered if she had once again been the victim of a long-tailed visitor. The longer she thought about the possibility, the funnier the idea grew. She imagined a possum climbing on top of the kitchen cabinet, grabbing the chicken, and dragging his prize past the sink. He obviously encountered problems when he tried to pull the chicken down with him, and the chicken had gotten stuck between the refrigerator and the cabinet. The whole family laughed over the mobile chicken as we imagined the thieving possum. At that point we still believed we wouldn't see any more possums.

Wrong again!

A few days later, I was taking a bath. Our bathroom, which wasn't much bigger than a matchbox, was the "lap of luxury." The rustic pine walls supported a matching, doorless cabinet above the open bathtub. There was no shower or curtain. There was a one-foot gap between the wall and the front of the bathtub. Another doorless cabinet pro-vided a modest storage area on the other side of the gap.

So there I sat, doing my thing in the bathtub, when a possum came strolling out of that gap between the bathtub and the wall. The second I saw the creature, I started screaming my lungs out. I'm sure I scared that poor possum worse than he scared me. He turned around and scurried back the way he came. I scrambled to the front of the tub and peered over the end, into the gap between the wall and the tub. That possum disappeared into a hole in the floor where the water pipe came up from beneath the house. That hole was part of the house's "venti-lation" features.

My mother burst into the bathroom and said, "What's the matter? What's the matter?"

"A possum!" I wailed. "He came walking out into the middle of the bathroom. When I screamed, he went back under the house through that hole."

My mom leaned over the end of the bathtub and said, "Well I'll be. I guess this is how the other possums got into the house."

I made short work of finishing my bath and cleared out of that restroom. My father repaired the hole. Our whole family laughed about the "late, great possum invasion" for many, many years. Looking back, I'm glad we were invaded by such docile creatures.

While our possum visitation was hilarious and still brings a reminiscent chuckle, I would hate to think what might have happened if we'd been invaded by a family of rattlesnakes…or a rabid fox. The Song of Songs states, "Catch for us the foxes, the little foxes that ruin the vineyards" (2:15). In context, this refers to things that can spoil the relationship between a husband and wife. But the parent–child relationship can also be plagued by "little foxes" that spoil what could be a beautiful experience. Our long-tailed visitors, while placid and harmless, were a source of familial upheaval for several days. Unfortunately, most "little foxes" might appear harmlessly annoying at first, but too soon they grow into mammoth problems that seem to be endless.

Bad attitudes or petty misbehaviors are some of the "little foxes" that can sneak into a home as stealthily as the possums slipped into our house. These taint our relationships with our children. These "foxes" can mature into perpetual, parent–child conflicts that turn into continuing battles that mar every day. Many times when parents suffer a lifestyle of conflict with teens, the "little foxes" were present many years before, but they went undetected or were ignored by the parents.

Adolescent eruptions are often rooted in issues that occurred during childhood. These issues can involve a parent who plays favorites, a parent who treats the child as a person of lesser value, unresolved heartache due to divorce, death, or abuse, parental neglect, parental stifling, or a child who is robbed of his or her childhood by excessive responsibilities. Some children try to tell parents about "the little foxes," but many times parents aren't in tune with the children enough to hear. Depending on the children's temperaments, the messages can come subtly or as loud as my screaming about the possum.

I'll never forget the time I was in the grocery store and I heard a five-year-old boy giving his mother a "little fox" alert. This boy kept trying to hug his elder brother. But the brother was irritable and repeatedly pushed him away. I noticed the mother gave the five-year-old very little affection through her facial expressions, words, or touches. Quite the contrary, every time the tyke tried to hug his brother and the brother squawked, the mother would whack at the youngster and crudely demand that he stop. I recognized that the young boy was starved for affection and was trying to elicit some form of human warmth from his brother. But all he got was more disapproval and more negativity.

In response to the mother's actions, the five-year-old always said the same thing: "I don't love nobody." I heard him repeat that sad claim about six times during a twenty-minute time span. But the mother never once acknowledged the "little fox" clues. The child was desperately trying to tell her he needed her or somebody to show him love, and all the while she was oblivious to his cry.

No one needs to tell us the probable outcome of this story. We already know it. By the time the boy reaches fourteen, he'll be running the streets. By the time he's twenty-one, he'll be in prison. And the same mantra that started when he was five will still be playing through his mind: "I don't love nobody."

This is an extreme example of the "little foxes," but sometimes even the best mothers can miss subtle clues. What are your children telling you? Have you taken the time to regularly sit in their space and have heart-to-heart talks about your relationship? Do you have the kind of open and free relationship that allows them to be honest with you? Even if you don't, I can guarantee your kids are dropping a few "fox" clues along the way. It's never too late to start looking for them. Even if your "little foxes" have grown to mammoth proportions, most kids—small children and teens alike—blossom when a parent takes the time to tune in, really listen, and respond in a positive manner.

SURVIVAL SKILL

For moderate wrinkles in rumpled clothing, set your hair dryer on the hottest and highest speed and target the wrinkles. For tougher wrinkles, tug the fabric a bit so that it heats with the wrinkle flattened. This is excellent for travel and for last-minute touch-ups when you're already dressed and notice a wrinkle in your clothing. The hair dryer does not work for really tough or deep wrinkles, but it is amazingly effective on rumpled cotton, cotton blends, and knits.

Never underestimate the power of a hug.

20

Kids at Risk

Sons are a heritage from the L<small>ORD</small>,
children a reward from him.

P<small>SALM</small> 127:3

Several years ago I took my children to McDonald's for an after-noon play time. We had just arrived in the playground area, and my kids had already shed their shoes and were acting like monkeys on the playground equipment. Before I sat down, I noticed a young Hispanic mother with a toddler and a preschool child. The preschool child was on the verge of a bathroom emergency and the mother was struggling with trying to manage the toddler while dealing with her other child's urgent need.

I watched and wondered if there was any way I could help. I guess she must have sensed my desire to be of assistance because she looked right at me.

I smiled. "Do you want me to watch your baby while you go to the restroom?" I questioned. I must look like the trustworthy sort. In broken English, she agreed and whisked her older child through the doorway.

After the toddler and I sized each other up for several seconds, I attempted to pick him up. But he whimpered, slipped right past me, and charged for the door. Before I could catch the little guy, he'd flung open the door and was hustling forward.

"Come back," I urged and tried to pick him up again.

He darted a glance over his shoulder. His dark eyes wide, he began to cry in earnest.

"I'm not going to hurt you," I insisted. "Come on. Your mommy has gone to the restroom with big sister."

That only scared him more. He began to wail as if I were chasing him with a chainsaw. The closer I got to him, the louder he shrieked and the faster he ran.

As the playground door closed behind us, I glanced over my shoulder. My kids were contentedly playing with no idea that their mother was racing after an unknown toddler. I didn't want to leave them unattended, but the bawling toddler didn't care about my kids…or the purse I'd left behind. He raced through the dining area and zoomed past the order desk.

I decided I didn't have any choice…I had to chase him. If he somehow wandered into the parking lot he could have gotten killed. With another furtive glance over my shoulder, I trotted after the toddler.

"Come on, Honey," I soothed. "Mommy will be right back."

But that only increased his terror. He kept glancing over his shoulder and shrieking like I was Godzilla intent on gobbling him up. The more I tried to convince him I was a "good guy," the more he panicked. Looking back, I seriously doubt the poor child understood English. No telling what he thought I was saying.

By this time, we'd rounded the corner and were going for the final stretch, straight toward the ladies restroom. His short pudgy legs were pumping. Every time I tried to grab him, he slipped out of my grasp and bellowed.

With a final lunge, he plastered himself against the bathroom door. While the door swung inward, he looked over his shoulder at me again, his mouth wide in a bawling frenzy. Fortunately, his mother was standing near the sink with her older child.

I shrugged and said, "He ran out of the playground."

With a smile, she nodded her thanks, stooped and picked him up. The toddler clung to his mother's neck. His eyes, dark and tear-drenched, focused on me as if to say, *Leave me alone you ol' meanie!*

I went back to the playground, thinking about the situation. Interestingly enough, not one McDonald's patron or employee expressed concern over my chasing the child through the restaurant.

That disturbed me. What if I had been a kidnapper? Would they have all just watched in silence as I scooped up the baby and left the restaurant? Probably so.

Every time I read another headline about a child who's been snatched, I cringe. With the new rash of young kids being abducted and raped, I am more protective of my son and daughter than ever. A few years ago, in our small town, a man took a four-year-old from her front yard and raped her. Oddly, the man brought her back home and left her in the yard. What makes this so scary is that we live in "Mayberry, USA." If this sort of stuff is happening in small towns, the risk in large cities must be horrendous.

When I was growing up, my parents allowed us to play in the front yard alone and didn't worry about it. In one neighborhood, we were allowed to ride our bikes up and down the street and visit our friends' houses. My mother did always insist on knowing exactly where we were. But that was around thirty years ago. Today it's not safe for children to roam—even in their own neighborhoods. Nevertheless, I'm continually amazed at the number of children I see who are running free, up and down the street they live on or even several streets over. Often these unwatched children are the ones who are the most at risk.

My children are not allowed in the front yard without adult supervision. Roaming the neighborhood on their bikes without my husband or me is not an option. I do let them play in the backyard. It's fenced and the gates have locks on them. They know if anyone strange gets into the backyard, they are to run immediately into the house without talking to the stranger. I still keep a close eye on them, even when they're in the backyard. They also know that when we're traveling, they are never supposed to leave my sight. And when we're in a department store in our hometown, my daughter—who is petite—cannot leave my side. I don't keep my son on as tight a "chain" because he's eleven and the size of a husky fifteen year old. It would take a weight lifter to pick him up and run with him. However, I do not allow my son to go into men's restrooms alone unless he has his cell phone with him.

Furthermore, I do not allow either one to go to any friend's house unless I am absolutely certain they will not be at risk. A few years ago my daughter became very irritated at me for not letting her go to a certain friend's house. I explained to her that there was a "situation" in that family and going to that girl's house was not an option—*ever*. Still she wasn't convinced.

Well, a few months later the man of the household became violent while the little girl had a friend over. The police were called. When I learned of the story, I didn't keep one detail from Brooke. Her eyes big, she said, "Oh, now I know why you didn't let me go over there."

Ever since then, she's trusted my judgment and understands I have her safety as my highest concern. There are only a few people my kids are allowed to spend the night with or visit alone. And even then I have told them exactly what child molesters do and the moves they make so they'll know when they are in danger.

The days of children being blissfully ignorant are over. They must understand that they are at risk and know what self-defense measures to take if someone attempts to assault or nab them.

Granted, I don't stay in a paranoid tailspin and make my kids neurotic over the possibilities of being kidnapped. But they understand the rules and they understand why those rules are intact.

What defense measures are you taking for your children?

SURVIVAL SKILL

If your school-aged children have to stay at home alone, lay down the law about what they can and cannot do. Make sure they stay inside and do not answer the door for any reason. Also tell them if anyone calls, they are never to indicate that they are alone.

Regularly pray for your children's safety.
Trust the Lord to protect and defend them.
But also pray that He'll give you the insight to know how
to best implement practical safety rules.

21

Longhorns and Love

*Immediately Jesus made the disciples get into the boat and
go on ahead of him to the other side, while he dismissed the crowd.
After he had dismissed them, he went up on a mountainside
by himself to pray. When evening came,
he was there alone.*

MATTHEW 14:22-23

East Texas is an interesting combination of high-tech metropolitan areas and tiny towns. In some of these small towns it's almost as if time has stood still. The small Texas town I live in is no exception. I often jokingly refer to it as Mayberry, USA. However, we do have our share of modern problems, such as drugs and alcohol and gangs. We also have our share of modern conveniences, such as a Wal-Mart SuperCenter. (Actually, our Wal-Mart SuperCenter is the center of culture for miles around.) But there are some things that haven't changed since nineteenth-century cowboys drove herds of cattle across the varied terrain.

In the wee hours of the morning, my friend Frieda, a single mom, learned just how much the Texas past still affects our small-town present. She awoke to hear a tapping against her window. Being a woman alone, she worried first for the safety of herself and her daughters. She stiffened beneath the warmth of her covers and strained to hear any signs of forced entry. Nervously she peered through the moon-laden darkness to catch sight of any intruder. After several breathless moments, she realized that the intruder's attempts to break into her home held a certain cadence. Soon Frieda figured that either the invader had a lot of rhythm…or the tapping entity wasn't someone trying to get in.

After screwing up all her courage, Frieda thrust her feet from beneath the covers, stood up, and walked across the spongy carpet toward the window. She bit her trembling lips, inched aside the curtains, and peered out her window into the darkness. Much to her amazement, she saw something far from human. She encountered a yard full of Texas longhorns. The nearest longhorn stood beside her window, and his tail flapped against the glass with the steady beat of a happy flower-eating beast. The longhorns not only took over Frieda's yard but also had stomped into her flowerbeds and were relishing the rare delicacies.

If you've never seen a Texas longhorn, they're best imagined by starting with a small elephant. In your mind remove the elephant's skin and replace it with white cowhide that has large brown spots. Take off the elephant's ears and give it cow ears. Then remove the elephant's tusks and place them near the ears. Elongate the tusks so that they have a six-foot span from one tip to the next. Replace the elephant feet with cattle hooves, and put an obstinate gleam in the creature's eyes. Now you have Texas longhorns! Contrary to popular belief, they're really not cattle—they're "beasts with a moo"!

These beasts with a moo were systematically destroying Frieda's flowers and leaving hoofprints all over her yard. After several stunned seconds, Frieda dropped the curtain, stood with hands on hips, and determined what exactly to do. She did what any other sane, independent, twenty-first-century mother would do—she grabbed her phone and dialed 911.

"Hello—please state your emergency."

"Well, uh—I don't know if you could exactly call this an emergency," Frieda hedged. "But you see, I live in town, right across from the high school, and my yard is full of longhorns." Frieda pondered her beautiful flowerbeds. "And they're eating my flowers!"

"Okay. We'll send somebody right over," the 911 worker assured her.

The good thing about living in a small Texas town is that the city professionals are probably about the most versatile of any in the nation. Far from considering themselves so specialized that they refuse to perform certain tasks, our police officers are jacks-of-all trades. They have to be! Who else would save a lady in distress from longhorns at 3 A.M.? Within minutes a police car, replete with flashing lights, came trolling up the quiet, dark neighborhood. Those cattle, having never seen such a sight, stared in stunned silence. Then they lowered their ears and trotted right back from whence they had come—across the narrow road, over the school campus, and through the open gate of the neighboring pasture.

Soon after that episode, Frieda learned that the high school agriculture department kept the longhorns in a nearby pasture as a special school project and that "someone" had left the gate open. Believe it or not, "someone" has left the gate open numerous other times since this initial invasion. Now when Frieda awakens in the early morning hours and hears evidence of the mooing, tail-tapping, flower-crunching beasts, she grabs the telephone and dials 911.

"Please state your emergency," the woman always says.

By now Frieda is well known by the emergency crew. She simply says, "Hello, this is Mrs. Scully. The cows are out again." Without asking for further explanation, the dispatcher alerts the policemen.

As usual, the police car comes humming down the street, lights flashing. And by now the cattle are adjusted to the routine. The second they see the revolving lights, they just trot right on back to their pasture like good flower-eating beasts.[1]

At times our children can trample our space as severely as the longhorns trampled Frieda's yard. A wise friend once told me, "Children are the best and the worst thing all rolled into one." One minute they drive you nuts, and the next minute they make you wish you had twelve just like them.

One of the things that has helped me have more positive moments than negative is to have boundaries. Jesus Christ Himself set an example for having boundaries. When He needed time to Himself, He communicated that to His disciples and didn't apologize for the need. As a result, the disciples respected His space.

In my case, it's not healthy for me to allow my children to trample my spirit and rattle my mind. I can make some choices that will keep our relationship healthy, peaceful, and productive. And, as the adult in this relationship, it is my responsibility to establish these boundaries and make sure my children respect them.

Following through with reasonable consequences when those boundaries are violated is also essential. Telling a child you're going to "cut her head off" if she does that again is ridiculous. That child knows you aren't going to do that. You will reap no change in behavior. Beating a child for interrupting is not only abusive, it is too much punishment for the act that was committed. The child will silently seethe and resent you, not respect you.

For instance, if my children are whining and pestering me to begin a trip to the store I've told them they can go on, I tell them, "If you don't stop pestering me, when I do get ready to go, I won't take you with me." Because I do what I tell them I'm going to do, they know this is not an idle threat. They stop whining. Peace once again reigns.

When we get to the store, if they start begging me for everything they see, I tell them, "If you don't stop, I will take you back home now." They stop. They know I mean it. We then have a more placid shopping experience.

If one of them decided to sass me in front of a friend to look "big," I tell them that if they sass me again they will not have a friend over for a month. For perpetually interrupting me while I'm on the telephone, I ground them from the phone for a week—after a warning, of course.

The only way to successfully establish and keep boundaries with children is to consistently enforce them. But a wise parent also gives the child the same respect. I don't nag or pester my children because I don't allow them to do that to me. I don't verbally mistreat my children in private or in front of my friends because I don't allow that treatment from them. I don't interrupt my children on the phone or in a conversation. My husband and I give the same respect to each other in front of our kids. We don't complain about, criticize, or disrespect each other in private or public. Therefore, if my children decided to be rude or sassy, I can say, "Your father and I don't talk to each other that way, and I don't talk to you that way. And I will not allow you to speak to me in this manner. It's time to stop."

Remember, whatever boundaries you enforce with your children, honor the same boundaries with them and your spouse in front of them. If we don't do this, we may spend our parenting years feeling like our own children are invading longhorns, trampling our space. This leads to resentment and a lifetime of dysfunctional relationships.

SURVIVAL SKILL

Baby shampoo is a wonderful facial wash that miraculously clears up pimples for teenagers, moms, and what is known as "baby acne" on infants' cheeks. Use it morning and night. Generic brands work just as well as name brands. (Note: normal, adolescent pimples and the tiny pimples on babies' cheeks are often called acne, but they are not true acne. Acne is a skin condition that looks more like a pit-causing, purplish rash of pimples than individual zits and often leaves scars. Acne should be treated by a doctor.)

While it's important to spend time with your kids,
it's just as important to allow yourself some "me" time.

22

Pickles and Post-Partum Depression

And she gave birth to her firstborn, a son.

LUKE 2:7

When I was in high school, I worked as a nurse's aid in the obstetrics ward of a hospital. That meant when I was the tender ages of 16 to 18, I watched women give birth. I saw the pain, the agony, the distress. I saw it all! I also helped in the nursery with the newborns. I had an early education about the upheaval of childbirth and the high maintenance of babies. Therefore, I decided rip-your-guts-out pain was one thing I just didn't want to endure. For many years after my marriage, I knew I could do just fine without the excruciating experience of labor. But after 10½ years, the baby bug hit Daniel and me, and we decided we should try to have a family.

One day before I even knew I was pregnant, we were in the grocery store. Daniel stopped at the pickle aisle and said, "Debra, just *look* at all these pickles. Aren't they just wonderful? Just look at them! There are all kinds to choose from. Hot ones and sweet ones and everything in between!"

As he salivated over the pickles in a way I'd never seen him do, I thought, *This is really weird!* But I said, "Yeah, they, um, look really good," while I eyed him.

After a season of deliberation, he chose some pickles.

I continued to think the whole episode was just *so strange* until I found out a couple of weeks later that I was expecting. Then Daniel and I laughed and laughed. Who knows what was going on in his subconscious. I've heard of men having morning sickness before they find out their wife is expecting. Maybe Daniel was having pregnancy cravings before my pregnancy was confirmed.

Interestingly enough, I never craved anything when I was expecting. I was too busy being sick all the time. Whoever called it "morning sickness" missed the diagnosis with me. I was sick all day long. The kind of sick that makes your skin take on a grayish undertone. Unfortunately, I only threw up once. I say "unfortunately" because I think I would have enjoyed the relief! In the middle of all the nausea, one decision remained firm. I knew I was *not* going to have natural childbirth. My motto was "Poison ivy is natural. Just because it's natural doesn't mean it's good!"

As a first-time expectant mother with eye-witness experience from that OB ward, I had mixed emotions about my pregnancy anyway. Oh, I was thrilled to think I would be a mother—on the days when I didn't have flashbacks to the harsh reality of the level of maintenance a baby requires. However, I was certain I was not ready to go through labor to hold that baby.

My husband, on the other hand, was so enamored with the prospect of being a new father he floated everywhere we went. He would testify in church about what a wonderful experience it was going to be to have this little baby. Daniel was in emotional euphoria.

I was a little less elated. When we went to Lamaze classes, many of the first time mothers would discreetly say, "I'm having natural childbirth."

Oh brother! I thought. *You can tell they haven't seen it all! Well I have—and I want drugs!*

One thing led to another in my pregnancy. Finally I was sentenced to bed with pregnancy-induced hypertension. Due to these complications, I began showing signs of an early delivery, and the doctor decided to induce labor. By this time my baby had turned into a kicking maniac. I suspected I was carrying a kangaroo! And even though I knew the labor pain was inevitable, by the time I'd been kicked crazy for months and months, I was *ready* to stop sharing my body with a Tasmanian devil!

Well, isn't this just great, I thought on the way to the hospital. *Hopefully by mid-afternoon I'll have given birth, and I can have my body back to myself.*

I looked at Daniel and said, "Believe it or not, I'm *ready* for the pain. I'll just be glad to get him *out!*"

By this point, we knew I was going to give birth to a boy. That had sent Daniel into another level of euphoria. He was so excited about getting to hold his very own son.

We finally arrived at the hospital. They wired me up to a variety of monitors and gadgets. All the while, Daniel was right at my side, pampering me, making sure I was comfortable. I was grateful for his attention. As the labor pains began, I wondered if I really was ready to be a mom. Once again I had flashbacks to the nursery where I worked in high school, to all the babies I had helped care for. Those little guys had to be fed and burped and changed and bathed and fed, burped, changed, and bathed. The cycle never ended.

At one point I looked at the nurse and said, "I'm not sure I'm ready for this."

She patted my arm and said something like, "You're going to be just fine."

Well, the contractions finally started hurting enough that it was time for my epidural. The anesthesiologist came in and did his thing so that I supposedly wouldn't feel the contractions.

Guess what! I still felt those contractions—every one of them in living color! I told the nurse, "I'm still feeling the contractions."

She called the anesthesiologist, who came in and patronized me to New York and back. He looked down his nose and said something like, "You need to understand now, Dear, you are going to feel a little pain."

"Well, it feels like hot knives are going through my abdomen!" I replied.

Even though he complied and gave me another injection of the epidural, he still acted like he didn't believe me.

By this point, Daniel and I were heavy into the breathing routine they taught us in Lamaze classes. I had my focal point they insisted I should have. It was a little stuffed, orange lion. My son's first stuffed animal. I focused on my lion and did the breathing routine as Daniel coached me through. For the smaller contractions, you pucker your lips and huff in rhythm. For the harder contractions, you say, "He, he, he, he." This breathing routine helps you maintain control during labor.

Well, I was having some pretty hard contractions by this point. We'll just say that epidural was about as effective as water for me.

Daniel was watching the monitor. He looked at me and said, "Okay, Debra, here comes another hard contraction. Look at your focal point and say, 'He, he, he, he'!"

I said, "Woo, woo, woo, woo!"

He said, "No, Debra, no! It's 'he, he, he, he.'"

I responded, "Woo, woo, woo, woo!"

Things continued to progress as nobody planned. My blood pressure went to stroke level. The nurse was thoroughly convinced my epidural was *not* working. By this time, the anesthesiologist was standing at the head of my bed. At last he was certain I was not just being a baby. I was having exactly what I said I didn't want—natural childbirth!

My son, Brett, struggled into the birth canal and promptly stopped all progress. With the anesthesiologist sniffing at my side, I pushed for a solid hour of horrid labor. Induced labor is much more intense than labor that comes naturally, so what I experienced was truly as bad or worse than anything I'd observed as a teenager. Since my blood pressure was at stroke level, the nurse was in a silent panic. By this time, Daniel was panicking as well, especially since the nurse wouldn't look at him. I think the anesthesiologist must have been pretty wigged out as well, if his obsessive sniffing was anything to go by!

Finally the doctor arrived. The nurse got him cornered and whispered all manner of urgent secrets at him. He wasted no time. He ordered the forceps and pulled Brett into the world. They say you're supposed to forget childbirth pain. Well, it's been more than eleven years since I gave birth, and I haven't forgotten one thing—especially not what it felt like to have Brett pulled from my body with no pain relief for me. I promise, it felt like the doctor ripped out my large intestine. It makes my skin crawl now just thinking about it. Awful does not even touch the agony.

"He's here, Debra!" Daniel exclaimed. "Brett's here!"

Brett's raspy crying brought assurance to the whole staff, as well as to Daniel and me. Everyone laughed in triumphant joy as our son displayed his high-volume lungs. They put Brett in my arms, and I encountered a blue baby. Really! My child was *blue!* His torso was pink, but his arms and legs and shoulders were as blue as a crayon. The nurse quickly explained that this was the result of circulation issues, and he'd be just fine in no time.

I responded, "I guess he can sing, 'I'll Have a Blue Christmas' and mean it, huh?"

Everyone chuckled.

And I fell in love. All my worries were over as I experienced an unimaginable, heavenly bond with my baby. He was the most beautiful creature I'd ever seen in my whole life. All doubts vanished, and I knew I was indeed ready to be a mom.

A nurse took Brett to weigh and measure him. I was wheeled into my room and was presented with my precious little angel. We made it through a one-night stay at the hospital and arrived home the next day. Daniel was flying as high as he had since he heard he was going to be a father. I, the former "Scrooge," was more joyous than I ever dreamed possible. All my fears were annihilated!

We made it through the first night, and everything happened about like I'd learned it would when I was sixteen. Brett kept us up nearly all night. But that didn't bother me. I was euphoric. In all my "Scrooge-ness," I had never dreamed the bond between a mother and child could be so strong and so wonderful. I was in heaven! Even after having only a couple hours sleep, I propped myself up on one elbow in the bed and looked at my baby, lying near me.

"He's so precious," I breathed before getting up and placing him in his crib. I meant every word of it.

Well, Daniel got up too. I noticed he was quiet and really haggard-looking as we walked around the sides of our bed and met at the foot. He wrapped his arms around me and said, "I am so sorry!" in the most pitiful voice I'd ever heard.

From that moment on, I watched my husband—you know, the guy who craved pickles—spiral downward into a severe case of post-partum depression. The poor man had been so excited about having a baby from the start of the pregnancy, and he was finally coming down. I, on the other hand, had been dubious about the whole thing from the start, and now I was ecstatic. While Daniel floundered for several days, I remained overjoyed. I never experienced post-partum depression. I guess that's the reward of being a Scrooge.

SURVIVAL SKILL

For new moms, those disposable diapers really do keep wet-ness away from the baby. I learned that I could let my son urinate two to three times before changing him, and he was still dry. That saved us quite a bit of money. Months after I shared this with a new mother, she told me that this was the best baby advice anyone had given her.

On days when your children are trying your last nerve,
sit back and remember their births or adoptions.
This helps you put everything into perspective and
makes you fall in love with them all over again.

23

A Lasagna Pedicure

And now these three remain: faith, hope and love.
But the greatest of these is love.

1 CORINTHIANS 13:13

Several years ago I "made" lasagna. That means I bought Stouffer's frozen lasagna in the grocery's freezer section and cooked it. That's hard work, I know, but somebody's got to do it. Anyway, this was a Wednesday evening, which is usually hectic for us since we attend a midweek church service. I rushed around to cook dinner so we could eat before church. After we finished our meal, I placed the leftover lasagna in the refrigerator. I was going to put one more item in the fridge before we headed out the door, but when I opened the refrigerator, the invisible fridge imps were at work. They pushed the lasagna right out, and it slid to the floor and spilled all over my sandaled feet.

"Oh no!" I groaned.

"What happened, Mama?" Brett asked as he rounded the corner.

Daniel was close behind him. We all looked at the huge mess on the floor and the generous helping of lasagna sauce covering my feet.

"We've got to hurry or we'll be late!" I said.

I managed to save the lasagna that hadn't flopped onto the floor. I left the rest of it—right there in the middle of my kitchen floor—for cleanup after church. Martha Stuart would *not* have been happy with me. I did the best I could to rinse off my feet and sponge my sandals clean. Then we darted out the door for the Wednesday-night church service.

We landed on the church pew seconds before my husband was due to lead singing. Shortly after the first song had been announced, I looked down at my feet and noticed a streak of lasagna sauce still claiming my big toe.

Oh well, I thought. *I'm sure no other woman here tonight can brag of a lasagna pedicure!*

Once we got home, I walked into the kitchen and moaned. "Ah man, I forgot all about this mess in the floor!" I know it takes a very special woman to forget the mess at home when she's got lasagna sauce on her big toe. Not just anybody can forget so thoroughly! But I did. Soon I had delivered the floor from its lasagna burden and my toe of the sauce. All was back to normal.

There have been so many times when I have dropped or spilled something around my house. Just the other day I opened the refrigerator door and a large bottle of ketchup fell out of the door where it was precariously perched. The new plastic squeeze bottle crashed to the refrigerator base and broke. Ketchup went everywhere. After I wiped up enough ketchup for a truckload of McDonald's fries, I found out my son had shoved the ketchup into the door and left it tottering at an odd angle. He has my "closet slob gift." What could I say? Since this was one of those things that wouldn't matter in a hundred years, I didn't fuss. I just asked him to please make sure he put the ketchup on the shelf so the bottle wouldn't fall out again.

"Okay, Mama," he said.

I can't tell you how many times my kids have had accidental spills and kitchen mishaps. I remember one time when Brett managed to flop out a gallon of milk from the refrigerator to the floor. Half the gallon spilled out before we could grab the carton.

I said, "Oh well, Brett, that's okay. Don't worry. Everybody does this at one time or another. It's all part of life." Then we cleaned up the mess together. I've used that same response with my daughter, Brooke, many, many times.

Any time I have a huge spill, like the lasagna disaster, one of two things will happen. Either Brett or Brooke will say, "That's okay, Mama. Don't worry. Everybody spills stuff. We all do that." Or I'll say, "This is the reason why I never fuss at you when you accidentally spill something—because I spill things too."

In order to grow up emotionally healthy, children need to be allowed to be children. One of the ways to do that is to continually remind yourself that your children are not perfect. They're going to have mishaps and spills and many other child-related issues. Wise mothers don't gripe about things children do just because they're children, including—

- getting mud on clothes
- digging in the dirt
- stomping through water puddles
- running through sprinklers
- spilling everything from dinner drinks to their whole breakfast
- forgetting where they put things
- having accidents in their underwear or bedwetting
- changing their mind about everything
- being whiny when they're tired

Always look to the intention of your child's heart and discipline for times when he or she purposefully disobeys. Everything else will take care of itself.

SURVIVAL SKILL

Wrap several rows of Scotch tape around your fingers, sticky side out. Then rub or touch the tape along any garment that has cat hair or loose fuzz on it. The tape lifts the hair or fuzz right off. Wide cellophane tape also works well.

My mother recently told me that when I was about three I poured several bottles of shampoo all over the hallway carpet. I believe God is using my mother's grandchildren to avenge her.

10 Reminders for Stress-less Parenting

by Brenda Nixon

1. All kids can and do misbehave. Find out what's normal for your child's age level.

2. There are no perfect kids. Allow your children to be human.

3. Parenting is a short season of life. Cherish each day.

4. Physical affection is therapeutic. Give and receive hugs.

5. There's humor (somewhere) in the situation.

6. It's okay to take a break—exercise, listen to soothing music, read a chapter in a favorite book, or enjoy a cup of coffee.

7. Talking to others can ease loneliness or frustration.

8. There are no perfect parents. Be willing to apologize when you've blown it.

9. Wisdom knows what to overlook. If it won't matter next year, it's probably not worth griping about today.

10. Count to ten and take a deep, cleansing breath.

24

When God Forgets

*For as high as the heavens are above the earth,
so great is his love for those who fear him; as far as the east is from
the west, so far has he removed our transgressions from us.
As a father [or mother] has compassion on his [her] children,
so the LORD has compassion on those who fear him.*

PSALM 103:11-13

My friend Molly lives out in the country. She and her husband have four small children, a couple of dogs, and several cats. One day their cat Sam came up missing. The kids had been worrying about Sam for quite some time, but Molly suspected Sam was no more.

One evening Molly was cooking dinner in the kitchen. An all-American mom, Molly decided to do something quick and easy for dinner, so she opened a can of Spam.

Her eldest daughter, Jolie, strolled into the kitchen and said, "Mama, what are we having for dinner?"

"I'm fixing Spam," Molly responded.

Aghast, Jolie asked, "You mean we're going to *eat Sam?*"

"No, I'm cooking *Spam!*" Molly replied, swallowing the hilarity.

Last night, I was trying to get Brooke to brush her teeth. Like all little children, both my kids would rather flop into bed than take the time to brush their teeth.

After she protested, I said, "Yes, you need to brush your teeth. If you don't brush your teeth, they'll start feeling like they're growing fur. Then what will you do?"

She said, "I'd pet them."

Children can say and do some priceless things that give you joy for years to come. But children can also do some things that need significant discipline. My husband and I have saved the paddle at our house for the really bad infringements. And then we only administer one or two controlled licks—just enough to make the point. "They" say that when your children are young you believe they're brilliant. By the time the kids are six, you're just hoping they stay out of maximum security prison when they're grown.

We've had those moments with both our children. Now that they're entering their preteen years, we're back to thinking they're going to make it just fine. But the years from two to about eight really left us wondering at times. Nevertheless, even when my kids have needed significant discipline, I'm committed to bringing good out of it. After discipline for a misdeed, I sometimes write down what my children did. Then I take them out the back door and sit on the porch steps with them.

Once we get settled, I wrap my arm around them and say, "Look, I've written down on this paper what you did. Now I want you to understand that it's all over."

Then I pull out some matches, catch the paper on fire, and drop it on the concrete. While the paper burns, I say, "As far as I'm concerned, what you did never happened. It's forgiven. It's not going to harm our relationship or change my love. I'm not going to bring this up ever again. It's over."

As the paper turns black and curls around the edges, I continue, "And that's the way God works too. Any time you do anything that displeases Him, all you have to do is say sincerely, 'God, please forgive me,' and He does. Then He erases what happened from His memory."

I conclude with an assuring hug, a kiss, and an "I love you."

They always respond with a heartfelt, "I love you too, Mama."

According to Genesis 1:26-27, men and women both are created in the image of God; therefore, I believe both mothers and fathers affect how their children view God. This understanding fills me with a deep sense of responsibility as a mother. I know that my husband and I both are shaping our children's view of God. Therefore, I strive to live and act godly before them. I also show them the nature of God in poignant and memorable ways they'll never forget. But in order for this to really work in beauty and truth, I have to have worked through my own misconceptions about God. This has happened as I have taken the time to read and reread the Bible so that I have a healthy concept of who God is, how He reacts, and what He is like.

Psalm 103 describes God as compassionate, gracious, slow to anger, and abounding in love (verse 8). This chapter further states that the Lord remembers that we are human and that His compassion is available for all who seek Him (verses 11-15). If you are struggling with your image of God, remember, your children's image of God is at stake as well. Psalm 103 is a great passage to read over and over again until you have thoroughly engrained His image upon your soul and mind. From there, He will empower you to live in front of your children in a way that will leave a positive impression they will never forget.

SURVIVAL SKILL

Many bubble baths can cause urinary tract infections in children. Girls are more susceptible than boys, but boys are not exempt. If your children enjoy bubbles in their bath, try baby shampoo, baby wash, or hold a bar of Ivory or Dove soap under the tap until the bubbles are plentiful. Remember, highly perfumed soaps may create problems.

God is in the business of taking our disasters
and turning them into triumphs.

25

When Rules Rule

He has showed you, O man, what is good.
And what does the Lord require of you?
To act justly and to love mercy and to walk
humbly with your God.

MICAH 6:8

Recently I was in the grocery store all by myself. In other words, I got to go shopping alone. This can be close to a spiritual experience for a mother! I was wheeling my cart from the health and beauty aid department toward the grocery department. I slowed down as I noticed a cart in front of me. In a glance, I took in a young mother with a small baby. The mother faced me. The end of her cart was facing the end of my cart. She stood still and looked up at a man. Her flirtatious smile suggested he was either her husband or a boyfriend or some-body she *wished* was her boyfriend. Her focus remained solely upon the man, and she paid no heed to her small baby, sitting unsecured in the cart's child seat.

Before I could even blink, the baby girl tipped over and fell out of the side of the cart. I garbled out an exclamation and stumbled for-ward. The baby landed on her forehead before her little body flopped onto the hard floor. Her terrified scream drowned the grocery store's shopping music.

My heart leapt. I grew weak and trembled.

The mother panicked and started shrieking something like, "Oh no! My baby! Oh my goodness! My baby!" She picked up the screaming baby and sat on the floor. She held the baby to her chest and rocked and cried, "How could I have let this happen to my baby?"

In the confusion, a store employee rushed up. "What happened?" the middle-aged woman demanded.

"Oh Mom!" the mother wailed and turned to the employee. "She fell out of the cart!"

"And where were *you!*" the grandmother demanded as she took the crying infant.

"I was right here!" The mother covered her face, hunched her shoulders, and shook.

Despite my pity for the mother and my alarm over the hurt baby, I knew I had to do what was right. I'd seen the whole thing. I turned to a couple of other store employees and said, "I saw everything. The mother was focused on the man. She wasn't watching her baby, and it wasn't secured in the child seat at all." I wrote and signed a statement to that effect. This way the store wasn't liable for the mother's negligence.

One of the store employees, who had medical training, expressed concern that the baby was showing signs of a concussion—crying with no tears. The grandmother and mother began to make preparations to take the child to the emergency room. In the mix, I learned that the baby was only three months old.

I pushed my cart past the scene and tried to calm myself. About thirty minutes later, when I was checking out my groceries, I was still upset and shaking. I asked the cashier if she'd heard anything about the baby, and she said no. Another cashier neared and said that the mother was only sixteen. I explained that I'd never felt so helpless when I watched the baby fall. And even though I pitied the mother, I was also exasperated at her for behaving so irresponsibly. She had flouted safety rules at the expense of her baby's health.

Safety rules are not optional at our house. We never have allowed our kids to ride in a vehicle without a car seat when they were little or without a seat belt now. We also didn't set our babies in a shopping cart and expect them to maintain their balance while unattended. We never left our babies or toddlers alone in the bathtub or allowed them to play with sharp objects.

All these rules have logical reasons for existing. Likewise, there are many spiritual rules, such as the Ten Commandments, that have logical reasons to be enforced. God didn't contrive the Ten Commandments on a whim. They are very rational. For instance, one of the Ten Commandments says, "Remember the Sabbath day by keeping it holy…the seventh day is a Sabbath to the LORD your God. On it you shall not do any work" (Exodus 20:8,10). Studies have shown that people who rest every seventh day maintain a higher level of health and work productivity. However, God created this rule for our benefit, not for us to be a slave to it. As Jesus so aptly stated, "The Sabbath was made for man, not man for the Sabbath" (Mark 2:27).

We, as parents, are responsible, not only for our children's physical safety, but also for their spiritual safety. While rules are important, God never calls us to create moral issues over optional choices. When we do, we become legalistic in our thinking. Instead of rules being intact for the benefit of the family and children, they become the force we serve. In other words, in legalistic homes, rules are in place to be served, not to serve. And sometimes they become a prime weapon for power plays and domination. When this happens, the children or people who are controlled are brainwashed into believing the legalistic parent or person is speaking for God. So if they disagree with this legalistic person, they are accused of disagreeing with God.

Consider some of the major traits of legalistic parenting and home life and honestly evaluate your own heart, life, and parenting for any trace of these:

- Picking and choosing key scriptures to support narrow concepts while ignoring any scriptures that contradict the concept or would bring balance to it.

- Creating parenting or home-life concepts that violate the teachings of Jesus.

- A one-dimensional thought process that insists upon one-size-fits-all concepts or is adamant in doing things one way only.

- One "God approved" method of discipline for all children, for all ages, for all occasions.

- One "God approved" method of education for all children.

- One mode of household management and revenue generation for all mothers and fathers with no thought for individual gifts. For instance, some men are excellent cooks, but legalists will insist it's the wife's "role" to cook. Some women are phenomenal money managers, but legalists would say money management is the husband's "role."

- No consideration for the events that real life can deal out, such as mothers or fathers who abandon, fathers with lower paying jobs, such as ministers of small churches, or the fluctuations of the economy.

- Viewing God as a rigid drill sergeant who doesn't consider the intent of the heart.

- Strict rules for nonmoral issues, such as style of dress and hair.

- Double standards, often involving boys and girls or men and women. For instance, moms are told to alter their lives/careers to meet the needs of the children and home but fathers are not. Or girls are held to rigid dress codes but boys are not.

- Breaking own rules on some level. For instance, telling children it's wrong to be rude and then being rude to children without ever apologizing.

It's easy to be legalistic because it takes less time. Legalists don't have to seek God for His specific will for their lives, their homes, their children, or how they handle their children. They just follow the list of rules, most of which aren't closely related to a moral issue. This puts the person who generated the rules in a god position.

For instance, I know a mother whose family was suffering financially. She was so convinced God would be angry if she even got a part-time job that the family stayed near poverty for many years. While it is highly important that mothers and fathers are there for their children to ensure their emotional health, it's also important that kids are taken to the dentist and the doctor and have proper nutrition and clothing to wear. Wise parents seek the Lord to find a balance that fits their families' needs. Please understand, I am not a proponent of mothers leaving their babies to another's care twelve hours a day. But I am a proponent of a mother and father seeking God's perfect will together for their family and children.

Unfortunately, the more legalistic we are in our homes and with our children, the greater the risk of losing them. Children often have clear vision because their minds aren't cluttered by adult complications. When it came to children, Jesus said, "The kingdom of heaven belongs to such as these" (Matthew 19:14). Kids frequently detect double standards, double talk, and violations of Christ's teachings. This can lead to silently seething children who grow into bitter teenagers.

Kids who grow up in legalistic homes often don't have meaningful relationships with their parents because the rules aren't enacted for physical or moral safety, they're enforced for control and domination. Kids from such homes many times are the ones who rebel during the teen years. Or they follow their legalistic parents' footsteps and remain spiritual infants for life.

Any time I feel like I need a spiritual balance check, I recall Micah 6:8, "He has showed you, O man, what is good. And what does the LORD require of you? To act justly and to love mercy and to walk humbly with your God." Then I remember Jesus' words that support this meaning, "If you had known what these words mean, 'I desire mercy, not sacrifice,' you would not have condemned the innocent" (Matthew 12:7). And I pray that the Lord will continue to keep me balanced in all things and help me not have a spirit of control, domination, or condemnation with my own children.

SURVIVAL SKILL

If you have left a load of clothes in the dryer and they've become wrinkled, put them back in the dryer with a damp towel and re-dry.

When we sacrifice our children's spiritual,
physical, emotional, or mental health
to keep "the rules," we have become legalistic parents.

26

I Am Going to Die!

Come my children, listen to me; I will teach you the fear of the LORD.
Whoever of you loves life and desires to see many good days,
keep your tongue from evil and your lips from speaking lies.
Turn from evil and do good; seek peace and pursue it.
The eyes of the LORD are on the righteous
and his ears are attentive to their cry."

PSALM 34:11-15

A few years ago I went in for my annual medical exam. My doctor began the usual series of questions and concluded by asking if there was anything I would like to discuss. I mentioned that in the last couple of years I had been awakened in the night a few times by an onslaught of tingles, accompanied by an inability to move. I was highly concerned. She was concerned too and recommended that I undergo a series of tests that included blood work, an MRI on my brain, and an EEG.

Despite my doctor's rush to order the tests, I was at peace. The peace didn't wane, even as I went through each test. I knew everything would come out okay and the doctor would determine that I was having some allergic reaction to my new laundry soap or something equally simple and benign.

Then the nurse called. She reported that all my tests came back normal except my MRI reflected an area of "uncertain significance." At this point, I was shaken. I began to fire a battery of questions at the nurse—none of which she was allowed to answer. So we scheduled a follow-up appointment with my doctor.

After I hung up I thought, *I've got enough sense to figure out an "area of uncertain significance" doesn't mean anything.* I soon deduced they found something and just didn't know what it was. In order to make light of the situation, I told my husband that the "area of uncertain significance" is where I keep all my books filed. He didn't think the joke was half as funny as I did. By now he was starting to worry.

Meanwhile, I was scheduled to have my EEG. If you've never had one of these tests, imagine a three-year-old taking pipe cleaners from the craft box and attaching them all over your head with silly putty. I looked like Medusa on a bad hair day. They say they're measuring brain waves, but I felt more like they were just having a good time making me look goofy. I went into that test figuring it would come back somewhat abnormal because everyone in the White family is a little wacky.

But I didn't expect the doctor to call me back that very evening. He left a voice mail saying he'd read my EEG and wanted to see me in his office. He said something like, "Not to alarm you, but I need to see you as soon as possible." When I tried to return his call, all I got was voice mail.

At this point, I was shaken to the core. I called Daniel into my office and told him everything. We stared at each other for awhile. Even though neither of us spoke, I saw in his eyes what I was thinking, "This is it, Ethel! I'm a goner! I'm outta here. I've lived my last year on planet Earth. *I am dying!*"

We started talking about my imminent death. "How are the kids going to make it without me?" I whispered.

"I don't know," Daniel fretted. "The kids are only six and eight! It's awful to think of them without a mother. I don't know what any of us will do."

We talked several minutes, discussed everything except the color of my casket, and stopped just short of wailing, "Oh woe is us!" and yanking out our hair.

Despite all the trauma, we put on a calm front and got the kids into their beds. Then we crawled into our bed. Before I drifted off to sleep, that deep, unspeakable peace descended upon me once more. I awoke the next morning realizing I had been blessed with a splendid night's rest. Daniel, on the other hand, barely slept and wasn't really impressed with my report of having a great night.

As soon as the doctor's office opened, I called them. As things usually go, I had to leave a voice mail with the nurse to call me back. When she finally got around to returning my call, she cheerfully informed me that the doctor had gotten my EEG reading mixed up with someone else's. She said, "Your test was perfectly normal!" I joyfully thanked her and enjoyed a wave of relief.

As I hung up the phone, I was overwhelmed with another emotion: irritation at the doctor. I called Daniel at work. He too was relieved…and exasperated. All that funeral planning and worrying had been for nothing. And to think I'd wasted all that mental energy trying to decide what to wear to my own funeral when I could have been planning my attire for my next speaking engagement.

The next thing on my agenda was a trip to my doctor's office. Shortly after she entered the exam room, I said something like, "Look, I know an 'area of uncertain significance' doesn't mean a thing. Level with me, okay?"

She explained that there was a bright spot on the scan. "Most likely it's not anything," she said and then started talking about Multiple Sclerosis.

Multiple Sclerosis! I thought. *This is it, Ethel!* Then, in my mind, I started clutching my chest and staggering around the room. I had survived the EEG, but I didn't expect to be so fortunate two times in a row.

I decided that while Multiple Sclerosis (MS) wasn't my first choice for the rest of my life, at least I *was* going to live. That cheered me up considerably. So did the continual peace that just would not stop. The doctor made me an appointment with a neurologist.

I went home and informed my husband that while his wife was going to live, I might be doing that in a wheelchair. We both decided to look up MS on the Internet. After exhaustive reading, we discovered that some people live with MS for decades and never have more than mild symptoms while others are confined to a wheelchair soon after their diagnosis. I decided if I was one of the wheelchairers, I'd just wheel my way through airports and still keep trooping for Jesus.

My husband and I still prayed that all would be well. While I know many women who live successful lives with MS, no young mother *wants* such a diagnosis. I had balls to catch and recitals to attend and errands to run and dust to bust. So we prayed. During all that praying, I was granted a perpetual outpouring of peace and assurance that all would be well.

Soon I visited the neurologist. After talking to me a while, she started making doctor noises. You know, stuff like, "Uh huh. Hmmm. Yes…go on. Right. I understand. Uh huh. I see."

Then she got my MRI film and scrutinized it. She pointed to my "area of uncertain significance" and said, "I really don't see anything out of the ordinary. This could very likely just be a scar. Did you ever have a fall as a child?"

"Oh yes," I explained. "I was involved in a car wreck when I was a preschooler. I was thrown from the back of the car and hit my head against the dashboard. Then, when I was a baby, my dad says I dove off a table and landed smack on top of my head. My neck bent back so far my mom was afraid I broke it."

"That would explain this spot," she ascertained and decided it was just scar tissue. She then looked at me and said, "I really think you've got a sleep disorder."

I thought something like, *A sleep disorder! Yes! Sleep disorders are wonderful. What a time to be alive. What a time to have a disorder. I am going to live a normal life. Oh, thank you, Jesus!*

She went on to explain that I was waking up during the dream segment of my sleep and that nobody was supposed to do that. The "paralysis" I was feeling was actually my body being in the natural state of paralysis during the dream cycle. Our bodies are programmed to do this so we won't get up during our dreams and try to act them out. Sleep walking is actually a form of a sleep disorder. The doctor further explained that the tingling was my body's resistance to my trying to move during this natural state.

By the time she got through explaining everything, I was in love with my doctor. I grabbed her and hugged her and told her how much I appreciated her letting me live a normal life. That day I experienced relief on a new level. I floated from the doctor's office, crawled into my van, and phoned my husband on my cell phone.

"I am so relieved," he breathed, and I heard the tension unraveling from his voice. "Even though I know they were thinking MS, I was still thinking it could be something deadly. All I could think through it all was, 'How will I ever raise these kids by myself?'" He then went on to tell me how much he loved me and how thankful he was that everything was going to be okay.

I truly felt cherished that day and oh so grateful that there was nothing seriously wrong with my health. See, I understand that my kids desperately need a mother, that my husband deeply desires a wife, and that my presence or lack of it will impact generations to come. I, as a mother, have such a haunting awareness that what I teach my children will shape not only their children, but their children's children, and many descendents thereafter.

Any time you are tempted to feel insignificant, remember your every word carries the weight of the future in it. Every day you make a choice to impact the coming generation for good or ill by the life you live, the decisions you make, and the way you treat your children. If you were prematurely snatched from this world, a gaping hole would be left in your place—a hole that no one can ever fill.

SURVIVAL SKILL

Many children wet their bed until they are twelve or thirteen. This is not a conscious decision on the child's part. It can be linked to an undersized bladder or a sleep disorder. Wise parents don't punish or humiliate children for things they cannot help, such as bed wetting. Consult your physician, buy some special night-time underwear to catch the urine, and wait it out. Most children grow out of the tendency by early adolescence.

No matter what happens, no matter how bad life may seem,
God provides peace through all hardships if we
take the time to walk closely by His side.

27

Discipline that Works

*Wisdom calls aloud in the street, she raises her voice in the public squares;
at the head of the noisy streets she cries out, in the gateways
of the city she makes her speech.*

PROVERBS 1:20-22

Laney is a strong-willed child. One of the traits of a strong-willed child is that she won't take anybody's word for anything. Laney's mother, Brenda, learned early in Laney's childhood that the best method of discipline involved allowing Laney to make her choices, then let the child live with the consequences of those choices. For instance, when Laney was three she wanted to wear a pair of warm, winter house shoes on a summer fishing excursion. "Laney," Brenda explained, "you don't need to wear those house shoes, Honey. They are too hot. Your feet will sweat. Then you're going to want to take your house shoes off. But the wooden pier is going to be really hot, so you can't go barefoot."

"I don't care!" Laney said with a determined lift of her chin. "I want to wear my house shoes."

Brenda started to make Laney change into sandals but decided to let her learn her lesson. "Okay, fine then," Brenda said. "But when you get out to the pier and your feet start sweating, you're going to want to take off your shoes. The pier is going to be too hot—just like I said. And I will not pick you up. You will live with your choice."

"Okay, fine!" Laney declared.

They went fishing, and the whole scenario unfolded exactly as

Brenda predicted. When Laney's feet started sweating and the dock was too hot for her bare feet, she immediately wanted Brenda to pick her up. But Brenda understood that living with the consequences of your own choices is the best teacher known to mankind. She also knew that if she picked up Laney she would be violating her promise not to pick her up if her feet got hot.

So she kept her word.

"Laney," Brenda explained, "I told you exactly what was going to happen. Now you have to live with the consequences of your choice."

Even though Laney was not happy with her sweaty feet, she learned her lesson. Now she respects her mother's opinion in what footwear is appropriate.

A similar situation happened with Laney and her breakfast. Every morning Brenda would get up and ask Laney and her brother, Tony, what they wanted for breakfast. Each child told their mother something different. Brenda would fix what Laney wanted and what Tony wanted. The minute Laney looked at Tony's food, she would start screaming like crazy because she didn't want what she asked for any more. She now wanted what *Tony* had.

Brenda, being the flexible variety, initially said, "Well, okay, Honey. If you want what Tony has, I'll fix that for you."

After this scenario was repeated several mornings in a row, Brenda realized she was being heartlessly manipulated by a five-year-old. She looked at Laney and said, "The next time you throw a fit for what your brother has after I fix you what you've specifically asked for, I won't cook your breakfast for you for a month."

In her mind Brenda was already making plans to buy child-friendly breakfast items such as yogurt, fruit, cheese sticks, cereal, and Pop-Tarts. Brenda believed making a child go without a meal was abusive, and she would never force Laney to endure such a thing. But she perceived that allowing Laney to be responsible for her own breakfast would teach the child a lesson she would never forget.

The next morning Laney did exactly what Brenda anticipated. Even though Brenda reminded Laney of the consequences of another fit, the second Brenda gave Laney her breakfast she started screaming because it wasn't what she wanted—even though it was exactly what she'd asked for.

So Brenda did what she told Laney she would do. She said, "That's it, Laney. You'll eat what you asked for today. Then starting tomorrow, you can fix your own breakfast for a month. I'm going to the store, and I'll buy you some things you know how to fix."

Laney's brown eyes sharpened in resolve as she lifted her chin. "That's fine!" she declared.

And it was fine. For several weeks Laney functioned well as her own chef. She enjoyed yogurt, Pop-Tarts, cereal, cheese, and fruit. Brenda had even purchased milk in small cartons, just Laney's size. Laney's strong will never wavered, even in the face of her brother receiving a hot breakfast.

Then one morning about three weeks after Laney became her own chef, she decided she was tired of the same menu. She wanted a boiled egg. The only problem was, she didn't quite know how to cook it. Brenda found Laney in the kitchen with an egg in a shallow pan. She was standing on a kitchen chair pushed to the sink. Laney had the pan under the water spout and was trying to cover the egg with water. But the pan was so shallow, the egg rose higher than the edge of the pan and the water wouldn't cover the egg. Laney was whimpering with frustration.

"What are you trying to do, Sweetheart?" Brenda gently asked.

"I'm trying to make a boiled egg," Laney explained through tears. "But the water won't cover it so I can boil it." A broken sob punctuated the child's claim, and Brenda sensed she'd made her point.

"Mama will be glad to boil the egg for you, Sugar, if you think you've learned your lesson and you won't scream and throw a fit when I give the egg to you."

"I won't scream," Laney said, now crying.

A wise mother, Brenda knew the contest of wills was officially over. She turned off the running water, wrapped her arms around Laney and said, "I know I said I wouldn't cook breakfast for you for a month. It's only been three weeks, but since you're sorry I'll give you some grace and go ahead and start cooking for you again today—but you've got to promise me you won't scream any more."

"I promise," Laney meekly replied.

After Brenda served Laney her egg, the child said, "Mama, is it okay if I ask for some salt?"

"Of course it is, Honey," Brenda replied through a smile. "You can ask for anything you want. You just can't throw any fits over it."

"Okay, Mama," Laney humbly said. And that ended the breakfast escapade.

Brenda continues to use these disciplinary tactics with her children and finds that they are far more effective in the long run than administering parental force for every occasion. Understand that Brenda protects her children's health and safety. For instance, she doesn't allow them to go play in the road just so they can learn their lesson when they get flattened by a truck. Nevertheless, she allows Laney and Tony to make unwise choices in the small matters if that's what they're determined to do. She does not rescue them from the fallout of those choices. If the children misbehave or verbally mistreat Brenda while she's trying to help them, she simply removes her support from the effort for a season and allows the children to suffer the effects of not having good ol' mom in the situation.

As her children are moving closer to adolescence, Brenda is seeing that not only do they appreciate her help, they also respect her advice. They're realizing at an early age that their mother has a clue and that they don't enjoy functioning without her.

The reason this method of discipline is so effective is because it is tailored after God's methods. He understands that experience is the best teacher in the world. So He gives us guidelines in His Word and explains the consequences. When we choose not to obey, He allows us to deal with the fallout of our choices. After a while, if we're smart, we start making new choices that are more in alignment with what's best for us now and in the future.

I'm convinced that mothers who refuse to rescue small children when they have to deal with the fallout of their "house shoe" and "breakfast" choices are the ones who are blessed with independent, mature adult children who support themselves. These successful adults are often the people who were allowed to learn the hard way on small things.

Mothers who repeatedly rescue their children from the consequences of their own choices often spend the rest of their lives rescuing them.

SURVIVAL SKILL

Place a bowl scrubber with holder beside each toilet in your house. This way you can conveniently and easily scour away a toilet ring at its first appearance—even if you don't have any bowl cleanser handy.

Mothers who listen for God's wisdom
often find inspiration and answers
even at the height of parental frustration.

The Cost of Raising a Child

The government recently calculated the cost of raising a child from birth to eighteen and came up with $160,140 for a middle-income family. Talk about sticker shock! That doesn't even touch college tuition.

But $160,140 isn't so bad if you break it down. It translates into $8,896 a year, $741.38 a month, or $171.08 a week. That's a mere $24.24 a day! Just over a dollar an hour.

Still, you might think the best financial advice says don't have children if you want to be "rich." It is just the opposite.

What do you get for your $160,140?

- Naming rights: first, middle, and last.
- Glimpses of God every day.
- Giggles under the covers every night.
- More love than your heart can hold.
- Butterfly kisses and Velcro hugs.
- Endless wonder over rocks, ants, clouds, and warm cookies.
- A hand to hold, usually covered with jam.
- A partner for blowing bubbles, flying kites, building sand castles, and skipping down the sidewalk in the pouring rain.
- Someone to laugh yourself silly with no matter what the boss said or how your stocks performed that day.
- For $160,140, you never have to grow up. You get to fingerpaint, carve pumpkins, play hide-and-seek, catch lightning bugs, and never stop believing in Santa Claus.
- You have an excuse to keep reading the *Adventures of Piglet and Pooh,* watching Saturday-morning cartoons, going to Disneyland, and wishing on stars.
- You get to frame rainbows, hearts, and flowers under refrigerator magnets and collect spray-painted noodle

wreaths for Christmas, handprints set in clay for Mother's Day, and cards with backward letters for Father's Day.

- For $160,140, there is no greater bang for your buck.
- You get to be a hero just for retrieving a Frisbee off the garage roof, taking the training wheels off the bike, removing a splinter, filling a wading pool, coaxing a wad of gum out of bangs, and coaching a baseball team that never wins but always gets treated to ice cream regardless.
- You get a front-row seat to history—to witness the first step, first word, first bra, first date, and first time behind the wheel. You get to be immortal.
- You get another branch added to your family tree, and if you're lucky, a long list of limbs in your obituary called grandchildren.
- You get an education in psychology, nursing, criminal justice, communications, and human sexuality that no college can match.
- In the eyes of a child, you rank right up there with God.
- You have all the power to heal a boo-boo, scare away the monsters under the bed, patch a broken heart, police a slumber party, ground them forever, and love them without limits, so one day they will, like you, love without counting the cost.

—Author unknown

28

To Hop or Not to Hop

*No temptation has seized you except what is common to man [and moms].
And God is faithful; he will not let you be tempted beyond what you can bear.
But when you are tempted, he will also provide a way out
so that you can stand up under it.*

1 CORINTHIANS 10:13

Early in our marriage, Daniel and I lived way out in the country. We were visited by all sorts of wildlife—everything from beavers to raccoons. We also enjoyed a wide and varied frog population—especially green tree frogs. Green tree frogs are a lovely shade of neon lime green. They also have suction cup-type feet so they can hang on almost anything for hours.

These frogs loved our home. They often rode on our vehicles' windshields all the way to town and back. We found them clinging to our back door as well.

One fine evening, my linebacker-of-a-husband opened our back door. Sure enough, a green tree frog was hanging on the outside of the door. But this particular specimen decided the grass was greener inside the house than outside. So he hopped from the back door to the side of the refrigerator.

Daniel and I both looked at each other in startled silence as a stunned, "What do we do now?" hung between us.

The frog didn't give us time to prepare a plan. Refrigerator life mustn't have been as promising as he had hoped because he immediately sprang to the floor near our feet. I squealed and jumped away.

Daniel slammed the door and stumbled backward. The frog bounded toward the laundry room.

"Catch it!" I hollered, never considering that *I* should try to catch the amphibian. After all, that's what big, hulking men are for—to protect women from wild animals and, well, frogs.

"I'm not going to catch it!" Daniel bellowed. "I don't want warts!"

We both laughed out loud. My laugh was the loudest, of course. I never imagined seeing my fearless husband balk at touching a frog.

By now our green friend had hopped into the laundry room.

I, being the innovative sort, grabbed an unfolded washcloth from the top of the dryer and tossed it on top of the frog. But that didn't stop the frog one bit. He kept right on hopping. Now it looked like the washcloth had sprang to life and was leaping across the floor.

"Okay...okay!" Daniel said. "I think I can catch him now!" He swooped down and scooped the dishcloth and frog into his large hands. With the grace of a basketball player orchestrating a slam dunk, Daniel pivoted, opened the back door, and shook the frog out of the cloth. The traumatized amphibian landed on the ground, jumped off the patio, and headed back into the great outdoors.

This wasn't my first indoor encounter with wild creatures. Many years ago, I worked in a store. One morning I opened the cabinet to retrieve a cup for some hot tea, only to be greeted by a nose-twitching mouse. Once again I demonstrated my bravery by screaming, slamming the cabinet door, and running for help to the store next door. There I told my friend Linda about the mouse. She came over to see what she could do. Looking back, I have no idea what either of us thought she could do. Nevertheless, we cautiously opened the cabinet door. This time the mouse was sitting in a china teacup. He propped his tiny feet on the edge of the cup, twitched his whiskers, and observed us with beady, black eyes.

"Oh, look at him!" Linda exclaimed in her sweet, southern voice. "Isn't he just so cute? He's the cutest thing I've ever seen!" She gushed and "oohed" for several seconds until the "cutest thing she'd ever seen" decided he'd been trapped long enough. He leaped straight for us like a cape-wearing Mighty Mouse.

Linda and I, being the courageous sorts, screamed like the beast had landed in our hair. We nearly knocked each other silly trying to get away from that mouse. By the time the terrified critter was running out of the kitchenette and down the building's hallway, we realized we were hanging onto the cabinets like a couple of tree frogs. We were in a variety of positions all at once, holding ourselves up off the floor. After we looked at each other for a few seconds, we broke into teary-eyed laughter and got down from the cabinets.

What is it about wildlife that makes them think they're going to like the indoors better than the outdoors? I guess houses and businesses look very appealing to mice and frogs and lizards and the like—especially when there's tempting food involved. But the truth is, the poor things usually get caught in a trap, smashed, poisoned, or killed by the resident cat.

So many times wives and moms act like the frogs and mouse. They become restless and disenchanted with their world and feel they'd like to develop a new life elsewhere…alone. More and more often, I hear stories of mothers who leave their children and husbands. Sometimes the kids are young; sometimes they're teens. The husband is brokenhearted.

If you find yourself feeling trapped, understand that the Lord can and will offer a logical resolution or an alternative to abandoning your family. I never encourage a woman and her children to remain in an abusive situation. There are hotlines that offer help to battered families. If you find yourself in such a situation, I urge you to make the call.

But too many times the scenario simply involves a mother who's tired of being a wife and mom. She grows overburdened and weary and doesn't feel as if anyone in the household cares for her needs. The junior-higher is yelling at her while the preschooler throws a tantrum and the second-grader tries to flush the neighbor's cat. The husband comes home from a long day at work, plops in his recliner, and grumbles, "What's for dinner?" while never taking his gaze from the newspaper or TV. And he still hasn't realized he forgot her birthday two weeks ago. After years of such situations, some mothers start looking at their single, childless friends and decide their lives are much less complicated and more attractive. Finally these moms decide they can't take any more. So they pack their bags, write a note, and run.

If you're feeling the pressures of a less-than-ideal marriage and home life, consider making changes in the situations rather than giving up on your family. Sometimes moms need to sit down and plan a strategy that will change the course of their lives. And sometimes they need solitude to do that.

If you're truly struggling with the desire to leave, why not plan a weekend away—just for yourself—and use the silence to regain your focus? Remind yourself of all the reasons you're a mother or wife or both. Think what it would have done to you if your mother had abandoned you. Or, if she did abandon you, do you really want to do that to your children? Take time to encounter God and have Him show you how He can change you so you can facilitate a change in your situation.

So many times women become convinced that the only way to resolve a less-than-enchanting situation is to leave. But in reality, leaving often creates even more problems—like children who are wounded for life and regretful moms who find out the second...or third...husband is even less exciting than the first.

SURVIVAL SKILL

Ammonia and water is a cheap and excellent cleaning solution. Mix 1 part ammonia to 3 parts water for windows, mirrors, and bathroom fixtures. For mopping, mix approximately 1 part ammonia to 6 parts water.

Prayer changes you, and you change things.
—OSWALD CHAMBERS

29

The Serpents Among Us

Now the serpent was more crafty than any of the wild animals the LORD God had made.

GENESIS 3:1

Many years ago, when Robin Lee Hatcher's daughters were about six and four, their neighbor's son (around age twenty) had a boa constrictor for a pet. The son ended up in trouble with the law and was incarcerated. The boa decided it didn't want to wait for his release and escaped that fall. The mother went around to all the neighbors to report the missing reptile. Robin and her family looked all over their backyard, including in the trees and under the shrubs. No snake.

One day the following spring, Robin was going up the steps from the game room (converted from the carport the previous year) into the kitchen, and she saw something odd in a half-open box near the outside door. She stepped closer and screamed. That "something odd" was the boa, all six to eight feet of him. Seeking a place of warmth, he'd curled up tight on top of some old sheets. Later she also found the skin the snake had shed, letting them know he'd been their guest throughout the winter. Robin's imagination went wild because of how close that boa had come to being inside her home. Fortunately, a local pet store found the snake a new place, far away from Robin's home.[1]

My friend Joy Anderson had an encounter with a snake in her carport as well. She was going to pick up her eldest daughter from school one day while trying to manage her two younger daughters. After bathing the toddler, Grace, she grabbed her purse and started heading to the door. When she realized she didn't have her keys, she told her middle daughter, Amanda (age nine), to go ahead and get herself and the baby into the car.

Seconds later, Joy darted into the garage. When she caught sight of something long and unusual near the toddler, she immediately looked at the "unusual" again. In a heart-stopping second she realized Grace was toddling only two feet from a huge rattlesnake.

Joy did what any independent, strong, composed, twenty-first-century mother would do: She started screaming, "Snake! Snake! Snake! Snake!" She grabbed the baby and instructed her other daughter to come back into the house.

By then her husband, Randy, was alerted and prepared for action. He'd been sick in bed and was still in his pajamas, but that didn't stop him. He marched into the garage equipped with a hoe. He realized he was going to need help to deal with this oversized critter.

"Bring me my cell phone!" he bellowed.

Meanwhile, Amanda started crying because she just knew her pajama-clad daddy was going to get bitten by that mean old rattle-snake. Joy assured her daughter that Randy was going to be okay.

"I'm going to pick up Rachel," she explained to her husband, "then I'm going to Wal-Mart. I'm not coming back home until that snake is dead!"

Finally, Randy's friend arrived and the two men ended the huge snake's life. At closer inspection, they discovered the serpent had a rattle ten buttons long. He had been around many years. According to the residents of this small central Texas town, no one ever remembers seeing a rattlesnake before this one.[2]

I've had many encounters with snakes during my life—so many in fact that I learned to kill them myself. Eighteen years ago, Daniel and I bought a beautiful brick home on five acres of land. After we'd been there a few years, we realized the snakes were nearly as plentiful as the birds. And these weren't just harmless garden snakes. We had close encounters with copperheads, water moccasins, and even a coral snake—all of which can be deadly.

Finally Daniel and I decided it would be wise for me to learn how to use his .410 gauge shotgun. So I did. Any time there was a poisonous snake around the yard and I was alone, I'd go get the .410 and blow the thing to smithereens.

Then we had our son, Brett. The closer he grew to being a toddler, the more nervous I became over our reptile population. I had visions of Brett tottering around the front yard, bending over to pick up the "pretty orange rope," only to be bitten by a copperhead. Daniel and I decided we had to move.

Soon after our move, the people to whom we sold our house reported that a copperhead had invaded their home. Sharon said that her sons came charging into her bedroom one day screaming, "Mama! A snake is hanging in the front door."

"A snake?" she scoffed and walked into the living room. Through the shadows, she spotted what they thought was a snake and decided it was just a piece of door insulation that had come loose and flopped inside. When she approached it, the "door insulation" lifted its head.

"It's a copperhead!" Sharon screamed, realizing only about three inches of the snake's tail was trapped in the door so he hung head down.

She retrieved a small hatchet and managed to kill the thing while it repeatedly struck at her. In the aftermath, Sharon and her husband decided the copperhead must have been crawling along the bricks when he was leaving for work early that morning. When her husband opened the front door, the snake meandered through the opening. The serpent didn't get all the way into the house before the door closed on the very end of his tail. There he hung until the boys spotted him. It's a miracle he didn't get all the way in and hide inside.

As mothers we will face any odds to protect our children. We'll snatch them from the danger of a huge rattler or take on a snake with a shotgun or a hatchet. But most of the time the "serpents" our children face aren't as blatant as a rattlesnake in the garage. If we aren't careful, they'll sneak into our kids' lives and poison their youth before we realize what happened.

Some "serpents" attack our children's self esteem. Others tempt them to partake of cigarettes, alcohol, or drugs. Then there are the "snakes" that lure our kids to compromise their morals. Many of these issues start subtly with kids in their preteen years. Peer pressure mounts. Children are compelled to dress or look a certain way to "fit in." They're told through innuendo they won't be cool if they don't contaminate their bodies with substances. Or they're gradually introduced to pornography at a young age and seduced by peers or adults.

Many mothers do a good job of protecting their kids when they know the threat is on. Unfortunately, sometimes the best moms can miss the clues that their children are in deadly situations. Often mothers who adamantly protect their children from abusive adults don't realize that kids can do awful things to other kids.

In order to make sure my children are protected, I keep our relationship safe and open so they feel free to talk to me about anything. We have what we call "our special day" when I take out one of my children for a "date." We sit in a restaurant, hold hands, and talk about life. Many times I say something like, "Is there anything we need to talk about?" or "What about our relationship? Is there anything we need to discuss that will make our relationship stronger?" Sometimes my kids will share a disappointment I've caused them that I never realized. Sometimes they'll discuss something that's troubling them with a friend. Other times they're just happy to be with me and talk about their plans for the future or what they're thinking these days.

But I don't wait until we have "our special day" to make sure the lines of communication are thriving. Often at night I lie down with my son and daughter and spend quality time listening to them. They tell me if something is bothering them, such as another child saying something that hurt their self-esteem. When this happens, we discuss why that person might have felt the need to be so cruel. I also provide my children with some tools to manage that person, such as not playing into the hands of a manipulator.

In order to protect my children from molestation by other children, I don't allow them to take baths with friends unless they're wearing swimsuits. I don't let children play alone in a room unless the door is open. Even then I keep a close check to make certain no one is "experimenting" with something they've heard from an elder sibling or friend. I also explained sexuality to my children at an early age (eight and just turned nine). But even before they knew the whole story about "the birds and the bees," I told them the moves people make if they're wanting to victimize them. The days for silence are over. Pretending like these "serpents" don't exist in our world doesn't protect children in this day and age.

As for other serpents—drugs, alcohol, and cigarettes—I have told my kids since they were old enough to talk that these items would harm their bodies. I've explained that a lot of people who become addicted to substances wish they'd never started but they can't break away. While I never condemn people who are addicted to any substance, I also speak truthfully with my children.

The time to deal with the serpents society throws at our children is not when the kids reach their teen or preteen years and the serpents are blatantly present. It's in the elementary years—from kindergarten on—when the serpents may not be detected. If a mother has done her job well, by the time these subtle serpents become blatant, the child is well-equipped to overcome and persevere. The key to success involves parents treating their children with a respect that keeps their spirits open and honest communication flowing.

SURVIVAL SKILL

If you live in an area populated by snakes, get a few cats. Snakes and cats are natural enemies because cats will eat snakes. (If you need a cat, I can Fed-Ex you one. I still have five!)

There's no substitute for a mother
who listens to her children.

30

Mom Time

You prepare a table before me.

<small>Psalm 23:5</small>

Philip Attebery says that during the first several years of his parents' marriage, his father finished graduate school and doctoral work at a couple of state universities. Like many newlyweds, the couple struggled financially. They were not able to have much of a social life during those years. They could afford to go see a movie but not to hire a babysitter for Philip and his sister. They could afford to hire a babysitter but not afford to do anything if they did. The result was pretty much a stay-at-home situation for Philip's mom. She stayed at home, did housework, and took care of her lovely children. As outstanding as the kids were, they did not provide her with much adult companionship.

Philip's father, however, was able to get out regularly to the university. He was a scientist and able to conduct numerous fascinating lab experiments as part of his education. So while he was often out learning new things and seeing the world, Philip's mother was constantly at home.

His father finally graduated and was immediately hired as a professor at another university. Obviously Philip's parents' income increased and brought with it the possibility of an improved social life for his mother. After several months, however, she realized that their pattern of life had remained very similar to the previous years. She was at home with the kids every day while her husband was interacting with other people. As she pondered this situation one Friday afternoon, she devised a plan that would encourage her husband to take the family out for dinner. She intentionally left meat in the freezer and did not prepare the usual evening meal. When her husband arrived home from work, she casually let him know that nothing had been thawed out and that dinner was not prepared.

Rather than taking the hint and offering to go out for dinner, he simply sighed and said, "Okay, I'll go to the grocery store and buy something for you to cook."

This was more than the lady could take. She entered into a fervent monologue that went something like this, "John, I want to go somewhere! I have stayed home with the kids all week while you've been able to get out and do things. I've waited all these years for you to finish school so that opportunities would come to get out and go places once in a while, and I want to go somewhere!"

She remembers feeling such relief when she saw the genuine smile and expression of understanding that appeared on her husband's face…the look that told her he had indeed understood her pain. He began to remove his coat and sincerely spoke to her, "Okay, Honey, you can go to the store." This time she began another passionate statement that could in no way be misinterpreted. She had a driving need for the whole family to eat a meal *she* didn't prepare. Within the hour the family was eating the first of many Friday night chili dogs at a local hamburger joint.

In past years, many women found themselves feeling trapped at home. With no outlet for socialization, some of these women resented their husbands for not understanding. Even today, some stay-at-home moms feel as if one day bleeds into another in an endless cycle of doing laundry, washing dishes, and chasing after toddlers.

When Brett was a baby, even though I was a part-time graduate student, there were some days I felt as if the world were marching on without me—especially when I didn't get a shower until after my husband arrived home from work. I can't imagine how I would have felt if I didn't have at least the outlet of graduate school.

I recall driving the nearly one hour to my weekly class, sitting through the 1½-hour class, then driving back home. That gave me 3½ hours alone every week—just enough time to reestablish my equilibrium. It wasn't that I didn't enjoy being the mother of a young child.

I'd never been so happy in my whole life. Nevertheless, having time to pursue something that was my very own and that contributed to my personal growth was invaluable to me.

When Brett was fourteen months old, I had an opportunity to teach at a private Christian school for two hours a day. Even though I went for the job interview, I was convinced this couldn't be God's will since I had a young child. After a lot of soul searching, I realized the Lord was prompting me to take the position. On top of that, my aunt (my son's great aunt), offered to come to my home and watch my son for a reasonable amount of money. The second year I taught, my mother-in-law kept my son for free. You can't beat a deal like that! Those two hours a day gave me an outlet for creativity and communication and interaction. It also provided the little bit of extra income the Lord knew we were going to need.

What kind of an outlet do you have? If you're a full-time, stay-at-home mom, your experience will be sweeter if you have something you can call your own. Maybe it's a mother's group you regularly attend. Perhaps it's a night class you monitor or take for credit. It could be a part-time job for four hours on Saturday. Or maybe it's one evening a week at the library—just you and the books and nobody to disturb you.

Everybody needs an outlet—especially moms! I've found that I'm much sweeter and patient if I have some regular breathing room. If you're feeling cornered, take control of the situation. Just because you're committed to your family doesn't mean you have to ignore your own well-being.

SURVIVAL SKILL

Many nail salons use a quick-dry solution on top of wet nail polish to help the manicure dry faster. Essentially, this is an oil-based product that stops the wet polish from being easily marred. Baby oil works just as well and is much less expensive. After painting your fingernails, drench a cotton ball in baby oil and squeeze the excess over your wet nail polish. Just like the quick-dry solution, the baby oil will create a barrier over the polish that prevents it from being scarred.

Moms give all day long so we need to feel pampered at times.
Don't feel guilty if you stretch the budget for a nice meal out.
The price is a small one to pay for the stress-relief of
watching someone else "prepare a table before you."

31

Mommy Mouse

Come to me, all you who are weary and burdened,
and I will give you rest.
Take my yoke upon you and learn from me,
for I am gentle and humble in heart,
and you will find rest for your souls.
For my yoke is easy and my
burden is light.

MATTHEW 11:28-30

Kim Sawyer eagerly anticipated the birth of her first child. Even though the house she and her husband rented was small and nondescript and their funds were sorely limited, Kim had done her best to make the nursery a cheerful place. Homemade curtains and wall-hangings in pastel ginghams dressed the windows and walls. The secondhand crib held more gingham in the crib-bumper and appliquéd quilt. Things were looking up.

As Kim scuffed her foot across the scarred linoleum floor, she wished there was carpet in the room. She knew they couldn't afford it. They couldn't even buy a large throw-rug. But earlier that day Kim discovered a roll of leftover carpet in the storage shed behind the rental house. She'd called the owners, and they granted Kim permission to place it in the home. Kim could hardly wait for her husband to get home and roll the carpet across the linoleum so they could see the difference in the room.

After supper Kim's husband reluctantly trudged to the storage shed and hauled the bulky roll of green shag into the house. He pushed the crib against the wall. She stood in the doorway, hands clasped around her stomach and informed the baby, "Just wait. This is going to make your room look so much nicer."

Kim's husband stepped behind the roll of carpet and pushed it with his foot. As the first layer flopped open, a small ball of gray fur shot out from the green shag right toward Kim's feet. She shrieked and jumped. The mouse darted past her into the living room.

"Great Scott, what was that?" her husband yelled.

"Mouse!" Kim bellowed as she ran into the bathroom and climbed into the claw-foot tub. "Get it!"

"Let the cat get it!" he hollered back.

His fur on end, his whiskers twitching, the cat joined Kim in the bathtub. He was a brave, feline soul that must be related to my cat with hamster phobia.

Kim couldn't see what happened since she refused to budge from the bathroom, but the sounds told the story. Pounding feet, muffled yells, and furniture banging testified to the battle. Finally silence reigned.

"It's safe. You can come out now," her husband called.

Kim scooped up the cat and crept back out. "Did you get it?"

He held up a small corpse by its skinny tail. "Yeah, I got it." He threw the corpse out the backdoor, then looked at the cat. "Not that *you* were any help at all."

Kim and her husband headed back to the nursery where high-pitched squeaks greeted them. Kim's husband unrolled the carpet a bit farther to reveal a nest of pink, hairless baby mice.

Kim's heart turned over. "Oh, you killed their mommy."

"Oh brother," her husband said and rolled his eyes. After retrieving some paper towels, he scooped up the nest, babies and all, and took them outside.

Kim didn't ask what he did with them. The lump in her throat prohibited her from talking. She kept thinking about the little mouse family, snug in their home, their lives abruptly disrupted, then ended.

Her husband returned. "You're going to need to clean this carpet really good, you know that."

She shook her head but knew she couldn't use that carpet. From now on it would represent the tragic memory of the dead mommy mouse and her poor orphaned babies. As a mom-to-be, the memory was just too painful.

"Just take the carpet back out," she said. "We'll do without it in here."

He gave her a look only a husband can bestow when he's just man-handled a roll of carpet into a house and battled a mouse. "Are you sure?"

"Yes, I'm sure." She never wanted to look at that carpet again.

Her husband grumbled, but he rolled the carpet back up and hauled it out.

The room never did get carpeted. Kim also removed a square of gingham from her baby's quilt—the one she'd appliquéd with a gray fabric mouse. She never looked at mice the same again.

Motherhood is a unique, bonding experience that manifests itself with all mammals. Whether the mommy is a cat or a bear or a mouse, God has given her special instincts that kick in the minute the baby(ies) arrives. There's nothing more ferocious than a mother bear who believes her cub is being threatened. And there's nothing sadder than a baby left without its mom—even baby mice.

There are also few sadder experiences than a mother losing a child. I believe even animals mourn the loss of one of their offspring. When our cat Mamma Kitty had her first litter of kittens, one of them died. As soon as she was able to get up and move around, Mamma Kitty trotted all over the house, howling for her kitten. Within a few days, she began picking up the kids' beanie babies. The tiny toy in her mouth, she'd walk through the house howling in the same tone she did after her kitten died. That was about five years ago. She's still doing the beanie baby routine. My husband feels really "blessed" when she decides to howl all over the house at three o'clock in the morning.

Nearly two years ago, I rescued a three-week-old kitten from the middle of the road and brought him home. We named him Lucky because he was lucky he didn't get smashed flat. Mamma Kitty wasted no time finding a beanie baby. She howled all the way to her new kitten and dropped the beanie baby at his side. I wish cats could talk because

I'd ask Mamma Kitty if that was her adoption ritual. I thought perhaps she'd stop the whole routine, but she's still doing the beanie baby thing at least several times a week, and sometimes daily. I'm no animal psychiatrist, but I just can't help but think that Mamma Kitty never has gotten over the loss of her kitten.

Many women who have lost a child report that they never fully recover. Sometimes the death might occur as an accident, sudden infant death syndrome, death at birth, or as the result of a hard illness. Other times the loss happens because of an abortion or because the mother was addicted to a substance that harmed fetal development. However the death occurs, many mothers find themselves grief stricken, shattered, and laden with guilt—sometimes at the time of the child's death and sometimes a decade later. As the "what ifs" close in, the mother might feel as if she's drowning in a sea of regrets. Too many times well-meaning church people might increase the burden of guilt by their attitudes or by the very fact that the mother doesn't feel comfortable in sharing her loss—especially if she chose to have an abortion.

If you've lost a child, understand that God the Father endured the grief of watching His Son die a torturous death. He understands. Even if you are grieving an abortion, the Lord wants to wrap you in His arms and help you heal. If you are weary and heavy laden, He will give you rest and recovery. He will fill the void in your soul and help you persevere. Take the time to sit in His presence every day and allow Him to begin the healing process in you.

SURVIVAL SKILL

> *Redeeming the Past* by David Seamonds is a must-read for people who have suffered losses or endured traumatic childhoods. Please understand that any past, unresolved issues may detrimentally affect your parenting.

God has a special way of taking our grief and using it to help others.
This is part of the way He redeems our pasts for His glory.

32

Growing Slime

The LORD is my shepherd, I shall not be in want. He makes me lie down in green pastures, he leads me beside quiet waters, he restores my soul. He guides me in paths of righteousness for his name's sake. Even though I walk through the valley of the shadow of death, I will fear no evil, for you are with me; your rod and your staff, they comfort me.

PSALM 23:1-4

When I was about seven, my parents bought my sister and me a backyard pool. The pool seemed huge. Looking back, I'm certain it couldn't have been more than three feet deep and twelve feet in circumference. We spent many fun hours in that pool. I recall placing the kitchen chair near the pool's side and jumping in. The person who made the biggest splash won, of course.

I also recall stepping on a red wasp while my mother was adding water to the pool. The insect didn't like being stepped on and let me know with a hard sting on my big toe. To this day, I don't ever remember itching like I did a few days after that sting.

Despite this negative pool memory, once my son was two, I knew a pool was a must-have for him. So my husband and I went to Wal-Mart and bought a pool about the same size as the one I had as a kid. By the end of his second summer, Brett learned to swim in that pool. By the end of his third summer, he taught his five-year-old cousin, Ryan, to swim.

Now we've graduated to a bigger and better pool—a whopping four feet deep and eighteen feet in circumference. Yes sir-ee, we're in the lap of luxury! But it's sufficient to keep the kids happy through the summer months.

During the last nine years of pool ownership, I've grown just about everything but marijuana in my pool. Every kind of slime and algae known to mankind has appeared in the water. Once I woke up and looked out at my pool only to see the water had turned a brilliant shade of aqua. It looked like someone had scooped up the water from a pristine coastline and dropped it into my pool. Unfortunately, having aqua-colored water is *not* a good thing in a pool. The lady at the pool store told me it was some kind of algae that I had to kill or it was going to take over my life. I killed it!

Then there was the year we traveled to Vietnam to adopt Brooke. I was gone for three weeks. By then I'd learned a little about pool maintenance, but not enough to stop the water from growing enough green algae to start my own frog festival. If I'd thrown in a few water lilies, we could have been in the froggy business. As soon as I saw it, I knew I needed to drain the pool, scrub down the liner, and start over with fresh water. So that's what I did. Why I thought my newly adopted daughter, Brooke, would be content to sit in a few inches of water in her swimsuit while I tried to scrub out the algae is anybody's guess. Of course, Brett, then four, had an absolutely delightful time splashing around in the water. Brooke, on the other hand, just sat and screamed like a maniac the whole time I was trying to clean the liner.

Finally I got the liner clean and was able to drain out the remaining water and refill the pool. After a few more "green scene" experiences, I realized I could not keep the pool water balanced without some professional counseling. I took a sample of the water to the pool store and let them test it. They told me exactly what chemicals I needed to keep the water balanced, clean, and clear. Like a good little gal, I bought the chemicals and did what they said. Now I have my pool water tested every week or two, and I add the chemicals they prescribe. Even though I've had a few close calls, I haven't grown any frog-level slime since 1998.

Parenting experiences can often be like my pool efforts. We may start out with little knowledge about the process. Often all we have are memories from our own childhoods, and some of them might be as painful as a red wasp sting…or worse. We do the best we can through trial and error, but sometimes we still fail. Looking back, there are always things even the best parents wished they'd done differently.

If you're struggling with being an effective mother, there are many different parenting methods and theories available, from the most legalistic to the most permissive. In my efforts to be a good mother, I've consulted a wide array of books and listened to counsel from many different people.

I've learned that some people base their parenting model on one or two Scriptures while others approach the process with a balanced look at all biblical advice. Through my trial-and-error mothering process, I've had Christians suggest behavior I would never adopt. Usually they quote one verse: "Folly is bound up in the heart of a child, but the rod of discipline will drive it far from him" (Proverbs 22:15), and insist that children should be whacked every time they blink wrong. According to the *Reflecting God Study Bible,* the "rod" is most likely a figure of speech for consistent and balanced discipline of any kind.[1]

Furthermore, a shepherd in biblical times used the hook end of his rod to draw a wayward sheep to him, and used the rod in general to guide the sheep and protect them from predators.[2] Therefore, we must understand that effective discipline or parenting methods will draw our children and teens closer to us, not drive them away. This brings new insight and meaning to Psalm 23:4, "Even though I walk through the valley of the shadow of death, I will fear no evil, for you are with me; your rod and your staff, they comfort me." The best parenting and discipline methods bring comfort, security, and love to children. These methods protect children from their own dangerous decisions, and deal with any disrespectful behavior in a respectable manner.

In trying to be a good mother, keep in mind the following list of things that all children and teens need:

- **Basic human respect:** This involves not demeaning your child in private or public or talking to your child as if he or she were less valuable than you.

- **Unconditional love:** Regularly tell your children you love them just the way they are—weird hair, smelly sneakers, and all. I've told my son and daughter that I love them so much I even love the dirt under their toenails.

- **Preplanned, balanced discipline:** Decide what you'll do ahead of time so you don't fall into knee-jerk reactions you'll later regret. Time out for young kids is usually highly effective. As children age, grounding and taking away privileges often prove to be effective methods of discipline. Draw the lines, explain the consequences, and stick with the plan.

- **One-on-one time:** Take the time to have regular dates with your child and allot some at-home time to reading together or swimming or playing catch or doing your nails or working on a puzzle…whatever your child enjoys at his or her age level.

- **Affirmation:** Applaud your child for accomplishments and for things he or she does right. Don't offer critical correction on any offering your child presents such as a botched performance, burned cookies, or a crushed flower. Look to the intent of his or her heart and cheer.

- **Instruction:** Teach your children by your own example. Keep them in church. Talk to them about life. Don't wait until they are "in a situation" to deal with it. Think ahead to what your children will face in the future and begin equipping them to handle it now. My son is eleven, but I started talking to him about the teenage girl thing when he was nine. My daughter is nine. I started talking to her about the teenage boy thing when she was eight.

Dealing with our children and teens in an unbalanced manner can result in as much yucky slime in our parent–child relationship as I had in my pool. Keep your relationships sparkling clean and open by honoring and cherishing your children. You'll be surprised at the miraculous effects such Christlike actions will have on them—and you.

SURVIVAL SKILL

Mix Crisco (or any vegetable shortening) and flavored Kool-Aid to create yummy lip gloss for girls. Use old film cylinders or small empty cosmetic compacts to store the gloss for placement in purses and makeup drawers.

According to Einstein, the definition of insanity
is doing the same thing over and over again
and expecting to get different results.

Tips for Above-Ground Pool Maintenance

The following is a list of things I've learned from nine years of pool maintenance. We learned most of these tips the hard way.

- Follow instructions for setting up the pool, including treating the soil with a chemical weed/grass killer. If you don't apply the grass killer, the grass will grow up through the pool liner and create holes.

- Once you fill the pool with water, take a water sample to a pool store and get them to test the water. Most pool stores offer the test for free if you buy the chemicals from them. Buy whatever chemicals the test says you need and apply them as they say. At first I thought the pool store was just trying to sell me unnecessary chemicals. After I grew numerous batches of algae, I realized I should add the chemicals they said I needed.

- Don't ever use a flocking chemical or a filter helper chemical in a pool with a small pump. This product causes all debris in the water to sink to the bottom. If you have an in-ground pool, then you'll have a strong pump that can support a vacuum to suck out the debris. In a portable pool, the strong vacuum option isn't there so the debris sinks to the bottom and creates a gel-looking cloud. You'll never get it all out without draining the water.

- To clean your filter cartridge, attach a common, water gun/sprayer to your water hose. Turn your water on high and spray the filter. This is the only way I've found to thoroughly clean a filter cartridge. Just spraying the filter with water directly out of the hose doesn't produce enough force to get the cartridge really clean. Using the water spray gun method enables you to get much more use out of a single filter cartridge and save money.

- Keep the pool filled to the very top rim. This way the water level stays high in the filter and over the cartridge. If the water doesn't cover the filter by a couple of inches, when the filter collects debris the water flow is greatly inhibited and the filtration process is thwarted.

- The pool water test kits you can buy aren't as accurate as the test they perform at the pool store. Take a sample of water to the pool store every two weeks to test your chemical levels.

- Shock the pool with the proper chemicals after every heavy rain. Rain carries impurities and can increase your chance of algae growth.

- To keep your pool water through the winter, purchase a winterizing kit from the pool store. Follow the directions carefully. Cover the pool with a plastic pool cover. You don't have to worry about the water for several months—as long as the weather stays cold. However, it is best to take a sample of the water to the pool store in early spring—or when the weather starts warming—to make certain your chemical levels are still balanced. I grew a "wonderful" crop of algae late-spring last year because I waited too long to have the water tested.

33

Help! My Child Is Overweight!

The land produced vegetation: plants bearing seed
according to their kinds and trees bearing fruit with seed
in it according to their kinds. And God saw that it was good.

GENESIS 1:12

Before Lora became a mother, she would often see children who were overweight and wonder why their mothers didn't *do* something to control the children's weight. *Doesn't that mother know anything about nutrition?* she'd fume silently. Then she gave birth to a child who was born to eat. Even when Drew was a baby, he didn't ever want to stop his feeding time. As he grew into a toddler, he was like a food vacuum cleaner. Soon Lora realized that her toddler was a little chunky. She tried to moderate Drew's food intake and did a fairly good job until the child learned to open the freezer and refrigerator. Then Lora would catch Drew eating handfuls of all sorts of stuff.

Being a well-read mother, Lora initially fretted about love hunger—a condition where people turn to food to fill the emotional void left by a lack of love. Even though Lora and her husband both were highly affectionate with Drew, Lora upped the affection a notch. Nothing changed. Drew was still an eating machine. At times he'd even sneak into the freezer and eat frozen fish sticks.

For several years Lora grappled with the source of Drew's problem. Finally she deduced that Drew had a neurological eating compulsion. Furthermore, she learned that studies have recently shown that some people actually have a stomach pressure malfunction. Their brains never register that their stomachs are full.

This, coupled with the fact that some of Drew's acquaintances enjoyed giving him sodas and candy bars, created a hefty boy. When Drew was ten, Lora was able to begin reasoning with him about weight issues. She had several honest conversations with him in which she said, "Drew, you have a weight problem. I love you too much to pretend you don't. We've got to get a grip on it or you're going to grow up and weigh 300 to 400 pounds. Being overweight is not healthy. It can cause diabetes, high blood pressure, and heart attacks."

After several attempts at weight management, Lora got Drew to finally agree to try a moderate, low-carbohydrate diet. This meant Drew cut out all refined sugar and excessive starches such as most bread products, pastas, rice, corn, and potatoes. He was free to eat fruits and vegetables, as well as high-protein foods. This, coupled with a regular, reasonable exercise routine, has enabled Drew to not gain any more weight. Drew's dad supports him by eating a low-carb diet as well. The two guys in the family eat low-carb Monday through Friday. On the weekends, they eat what they want—within reason.

Through this experience, Lora learned that for some people losing weight is not simple. There are many factors involved, including metabolism and genetics. Some people just are not going to be thin—ever. Their bodies are programmed to be larger. While they can control their size to some degree, they still shouldn't set bone thin expectations for themselves either.

If your children struggle with weight issues, the following suggestions will be helpful:

- Examine your family's eating patterns. If one or both of the parents has unhealthy eating patterns, then the children might also develop unhealthy eating patterns.

- If one or both parents do have unhealthy eating patterns, be willing to change. Remember, Drew's father supported Drew by going on the moderate, low-carb diet with him.

- When your children are old enough to understand, begin educating them about what healthy eating involves.

- Help your children understand that this is an issue they'll probably have to deal with the rest of their lives and that you are trying to equip them to live a long and healthy life.

- Offer alternatives to every high-calorie food or beverage. With kids you can't take away something without putting something else in its place. For instance, instead of Drew drinking a sugar-based soft drink, Lora allows him to have diet drinks with Splenda. She also bought Drew sugar-free candy, and she doesn't ever cook desserts during the week.

- Be prepared to stand your ground in offering alternatives. Even though Drew agreed to the low-carb diet, there are still times when he begs for something sugary. Lora stays firm in directing Drew to the lower-calorie items. She also enforces this by lovingly telling Drew she isn't trying to be mean, but she's doing this so he'll grow up more healthy.

- Get your child into an exercise program. Lora and Drew walk and bike together. Even though Drew sometimes balks at the walking, Lora still makes him go with her. Drew doesn't die or faint. And Lora has learned that this is a good time for her and her son to talk about life, how to stay healthy, and anything that's bothering Drew.

- Unless your children are teens and as tall as they will get, don't expect them to lose weight. Just try to keep them from gaining excess weight. As they grow, the weight will redistribute and they'll thin up.

- Encourage aerobic play time. Lora encourages Drew to jump on his trampoline and swim often. These are things he enjoys doing, so he burns off calories while playing.

In America, more and more kids are overweight. We parents are responsible for not only teaching our children about moral issues, but also instructing them in how they can live long and healthy lives. If you have an overweight child, make the necessary adjustments and take heart in your journey. When Lora prays for Drew, she includes a request that God will help her, Drew, and Drew's dad in dealing with Drew's weight. She has seen a significant change in Drew's willingness to cooperate. She believes the prayers, coupled with her husband's support, have had a definite impact on Drew's attitude and success.

SURVIVAL SKILL

I often make a platter full of fresh vegetables such as sliced cucumbers, baby carrots, celery, and broccoli with a bowl of ranch dressing for dipping sauce. Then I casually set the platter on the kitchen table. Usually my children will come through and munch on the veggies—especially if they see me eating them. There's something about human nature that wants what somebody else is enjoying. This is also true of sliced fruit, melons, or berries. If I sliced up a platter of vegetables or fruit and said, "Eat these or else!" the kids would balk.

The more fresh fruits and vegetables you sneak into your children's diet, the healthier they'll be.

Things I Learned from My Kids

—Author unknown

For those who already have children past this age, this is hilarious.
For those who have children this age, this is not funny.
For those who have children nearing this age, this is a warning.
For those who have not yet had children, this is birth control.

1. A king-size waterbed holds enough water to fill a 2,000-square-foot house 4 inches deep.

2. If you spray hair spray on dust bunnies and run over them with roller blades, they can ignite.

3. A 3-year-old's voice is louder than 200 adults in a crowded restaurant.

4. If you hook a dog leash over a ceiling fan, the motor is not strong enough to rotate a 42-pound boy wearing Batman underwear and a Superman cape. It is strong enough, however, if tied to a paint can, to spread paint on all four walls of a 20 x 20-foot room.

5. You should not throw baseballs up when the ceiling fan is on. When using a ceiling fan as a bat, you have to throw the ball up a few times before you get a hit. A ceiling fan can hit a baseball a long way.

6. The glass in windows (even double-pane) doesn't stop a baseball hit by a ceiling fan.

7. When you hear the toilet flush and the words "uh oh," it's already too late.

8. Brake fluid mixed with Clorox makes toxic smoke—and lots of it.

9. A 6-year-old can start a fire with a flint rock, even though a 36-year-old man says they can only do that in the movies.

10. Certain Legos will pass through the digestive tracts of 4-year-olds.

11. "Play dough" and "microwave" should not be used in the same sentence.

12. Super glue is forever.

13. No matter how much Jell-O you put in a swimming pool, you still can't walk on water.

14. Pool filters do not like Jell-O.

15. VCRs do not eject peanut butter-and-jelly sandwiches, even though TV commercials show they do.

16. Garbage bags do not make good parachutes.

17. Marbles in gas tanks make lots of noise when the car is driven.

18. You probably do not want to know what that odor is.

19. Always look in the oven before you turn it on. Plastic toys do not like ovens.

20. The fire departments in many major cities have a 5-minute response time.

21. The spin cycle on the washing machine does not make earthworms dizzy.

22. It will, however, make cats dizzy.

23. Cats throw up twice their body weight when dizzy.

24. Any boy who reads this will try mixing the Clorox and brake fluid.

34

Picky Eaters Anonymous

Be as shrewd as snakes and
as innocent as doves.
MATTHEW 10:16

Beth wants to be a picky eater. I say *wants* to be a picky eater because her mother, Stephanie, refuses to allow her to be a picky eater. Stephanie realized soon after the onslaught of the picky-eater syndrome that Beth was using food as a control issue. In other words, Beth wanted to exert control over her mother and manipulate her to cook an extra meal just for her every night.

Stephanie saw through this act when Beth's older brother, Steve, tried it several years before. When Steve began sitting down to dinner and saying, "I don't like this," Stephanie, being the flexible sort, said, "Okay, I'll fix you some fish sticks or something." After a few nights of this, Stephanie realized she was actually cooking two meals every night. So she devised a plan.

The next night Steve sat down to dinner and began his usual "I hate what you've cooked" routine, Stephanie picked up Steve's plateful of food and set it on the breakfast bar.

"That's fine, Steve," she said, "You don't have to eat."

That was all it took for Steve. He changed his mind quickly and discovered that he loved the whole meal. Before dinner was over, Stephanie explained to Steve that he would eat what she cooked. He was allowed to have two items he didn't like within the sphere of the foods most people enjoyed. For instance, she never expected him to eat things such as liver or raw onions that many adults and/or children don't enjoy. She let him choose two things she cooked regularly that he would prefer not to eat. The rest he would eat—including green vegetables.

That ended the problem with Steve.

Beth was a different character altogether. While Steve was strong-willed, Beth had a will of marble *and* iron. When Beth sat down at the table saying she didn't like any of the dinner, and Stephanie set her plate on the breakfast bar and said, "Fine, then, you don't have to eat it," Beth wasn't fazed. She just sat and stared. One thing led to another. One parental attempt after another failed to end the Picky Eater Syndrome. The problem escalated until Beth manipulated the whole meal into a contest of wills over what or if she would eat. Every night, by the meal's end, Stephanie and her husband, Wayne, were both exasperated beyond reason.

The bottom line was that if the meal wasn't from McDonalds, Pizza Hut, or didn't involve potato chips, Beth was going to complain, ask Stephanie to show her how much she had to eat, and then argue and manipulate her way through the meal. Of course Beth always had room for dessert, regardless of how many times she claimed she was too full to eat her peas and corn.

Stephanie and Wayne wanted to be fair parents, but they soon realized that Beth was using the eating issue to control them and the whole family's meal time. They were also concerned about Beth's very thin frame. She didn't eat enough to keep a bird alive. They agreed to lay down a new set of rules:

- Like Steve, Beth was allowed to choose two things Stephanie regularly cooked as the items she disliked.

- Stephanie began restricting Beth's snacks before meal time so her stomach would be empty when she sat down at the table.

- Beth was not allowed to have any sodas before or during her meal unless the family was eating out. Then she was only allowed a few sips of soda before her meal arrived. This stopped her from filling her tummy with cola and then not eating her meal.

• Stephanie learned that if Beth regularly took her chewable vitamins, her appetite improved.

• Every meal, Stephanie placed a small portion, about two tablespoons, of each food item on the table on Beth's plate. That included a meat dish and two vegetables. Stephanie made certain the portions were conducive to Beth's tiny stomach.

• Wayne and Stephanie told Beth that she was going to eat what was on her plate. Furthermore, they told her if she threw a fit, complained, or started manipulative behavior, she would go to her room and sit until the meal was over. When everyone else had eaten, Beth would be allowed to come out and eat by herself.

• They also told her that the food on her plate would be the next food she ate. If she chose not to eat it now, she would have it later that evening or for breakfast. If not for breakfast, then for lunch the next day. Furthermore, she wouldn't be allowed to have any snacks until that food was eaten.

• If Beth was truly not hungry and wanted to save the meal until later, Stephanie agreed to cover and refrigerate it until Beth was hungry.

• On the nights the family enjoyed dessert, Stephanie also assured Beth that her dessert would be in proportion to the amount of "real food" she ate. If she chose to eat only half of her meal, then she'd get only half of her dessert. If she chose to eat none of her meal, then she'd get no dessert. If she ate her whole meal, then she'd get her whole dessert.

• Stephanie and Wayne made adjustments to encourage Beth to eat. They sometimes played the spoon airplane game at the table—pretending the spoonful of green beans was flying around the table to land in her mouth. And they often said things like, "Look, Daddy's eating his corn. Mom's eating her corn. Why not take a bite when we do: 1, 2, 3, BITE!"

• Stephanie allowed Beth and Steve to regularly choose a favorite meal. They chose a meat and two veggies to be cooked for the whole family. Sometimes they even helped prepare their favorites.

• On the nights when Beth helped cook, when the family sat down to dinner, Stephanie would look at Beth and say, "You worked very hard on this meal. Now how would you feel if I started complaining and saying I didn't like it?" "I would feel bad," Beth admitted. "Now you know how I feel," Stephanie explained. This regular conversation helped to underscore the whole process with the value of respecting another person's efforts.

After testing the boundaries a bit, Beth "miraculously" decided she wasn't such a picky eater after all. And Stephanie and Wayne learned that their child's being a picky eater didn't involve what the child liked or didn't like at all—despite the fact that that's what Beth claimed. It was all about control. Interestingly enough, gifted children are often picky eaters because they enjoy the thrill of the control game. Beth is a gifted child. And boy does she enjoy the control.

There are several keys to all this working. First, "be as shrewd as snakes and as innocent as doves" (Matthew 10:16). In other words, enforce the rules with love and respect, but understand you're the parent. Don't bend. The minute you give in, your child will start controlling your meal time again. Furthermore, you and your husband have to agree upon the set rules and enforce them as a team.

The parents also agree they will not use these concepts as a weapon of abuse. For instance, piling a small child's plate full of adult-sized portions of food and expecting him or her to eat it all is not rational or balanced. Furthermore, this is not a license to be legalistic. If Beth has made a good effort to eat most of her food and there are a few noodles left and two slithers of broccoli, neither Stephanie nor Wayne turn into tyrants. Instead, they see that Beth tried and they accept that.

Force-feeding a child is abuse. Know your child well enough to sense when he or she is truly not hungry. In those cases, allow your child not to eat but save the meal until later. God made food to end hunger. If hunger isn't present, consuming food is not in order. But be careful that the child understands no snacks are available until the meal is consumed. Once Beth fully realized Stephanie and Wayne meant this, she usually "suddenly" decided she really was hungry.

Keep nutrition in mind. Allowing a child to skip a meal and then giving in when he or she asks for chips ten minutes after the meal is not healthy. Giving the child a slab of chocolate cake when the child hasn't eaten his vegetables and meat is also unhealthy. Furthermore, allowing a child to consume sugar-laden snacks all day is a sure ticket to her not eating a healthy lunch or dinner.

Remember, each child in the family should be expected to live with the consequences of his or her choices. If Steve chooses to eat his meal, then he is allowed to have his dessert—even if Beth chooses not to eat. Not allowing Steve to have dessert because Beth didn't eat and she can't have dessert isn't fair to Steve *or* Beth. Amazingly, Beth's appetite usually mysteriously increases if she realizes Steve is about to get his dessert and she won't get any if she doesn't eat her healthy food.

If your child is a picky eater, it's important that you understand and accept the basis of the problem. Your child's taste buds are not defective. The whole issue almost always involves control. Sure, children are going to like certain foods more than others. We all do. Unfortunately, none of us can have our favorite foods every day. We must learn to adjust our eating to the greater welfare of the family, the budget we're working within, and good nutrition. Kids aren't exempt.

SURVIVAL SKILL

The face of health food stores has changed. Many health food stores are actually organic grocery stores. These stores offer great, healthy versions of "normal food" and even healthier junk food. I buy all my meat and much of my fruits and vegetables from such a store. It's all organic with no pesticides added to the food and no hormones, steroids, or antibiotics given to the poultry and livestock. Costs are a little higher, but I save by buying in bulk. Also we'll save money on medical bills in the long run. The Amy's Kitchen* brand even makes kid-friendly food such as pizza, pizza rolls, real-fruit toaster pops without lots of sugar, pizza toaster pops, frozen lasagna, and enchiladas. Many organic grocery stores also carry cereals sweetened with honey rather than sugar. Crunchy seed bars serve as a wonderful substitute for candy bars.

Many illnesses can be prevented with proper nutrition.

---

* Check out the Amy's Kitchen website: www.amyskitchen.com.

35

Romancing Your Husband

My lover is mine and I am his.

Song of Songs 2:16

When my husband and I had been married about nine years, we owned a small, brick home out in the country. This house didn't have an over abundance of windows, and our bedroom window was covered in blinds and drapes. On top of that, on this particular night it was cloudy, so the moonlight was nonexistent. All that is to say, when I crawled into bed beside my husband, the room was extremely dark.

I lay there in the darkness for awhile and finally decided to snuggle up to my husband. I leaned over, puckered up, and prepared to kiss his cheek. But my lips encountered something I'd never encountered before. It was moist and hairy and just plain weird feeling.

I backed away and said, "My goodness, what was *that!*"

"It was my armpit!" Daniel growled.

At that point, I realized my husband was lying with his hands clasped above his head, and I had missed my aim. My nostrils were full of the essence of Sure solid deodorant. And the stuff was all over my lips.

"Yuck!" I shrieked. I sat up in bed and started scrubbing my lips with the bed sheets.

If you've ever tasted a green persimmon, you know what solid deodorant does to your lips. Essentially, a green persimmon makes your mouth feel like you've just been the victim of a dentist's local anesthetic. My lips began to take on that swollen feel.

I bounded out of the bed and into the darkness, scurried toward the bathroom, flipped on the light, and grabbed a cup. While I was drinking water, gargling, and trying to purify my mouth of Sure deodorant I also was attempting to get a grip on my grossed-out emotions.

Meanwhile my husband was lying in bed thinking, *What in the world was she doing? Is this something new?*

Soon he realized none of that escapade was planned. He also found out the about-to-be romantic moment was *over!* After going through that shock, I was officially *out* of the mood.

This botched romance scene occurred *before* we had children. Things were different then. We actually went to bed at the same time every night. After having a baby, there were many nights one of us would take the night shift while the other one slept. As the kids got older, I would sometimes use the after-bedtime hours as my office hours. Romance can be challenging when you have children.

During one of my regular checkups with my physician, the nurse made a reference to married sexuality. I looked at her and said, "How long has it been since you had a two-year-old? At eleven o'clock at night *nobody* cares. And I mean *nobody!*"

She laughed.

I recently read an article in which a woman of young children said that sex no longer existed for her and her husband. The truth of the matter is, if a husband and wife don't try to keep the fires burning in their marriage, the stress and demands of having children can sap every scrap of energy until there's nothing left for romance.

My husband and I have made many creative adjustments in our attempts to keep our marriage vibrant. We have arranged for trusted family members and friends to tend our children while we enjoyed our marriage. We've even stolen away for a few solitary weekends.

As the kids have aged past the baby stage, we put locks on our bedroom doors so they can't invade our privacy unannounced. Right now, the locks work beautifully. Once the kids become teenagers, they will probably be too much in the know for us to claim we're just lying down for awhile. But those years will lend themselves to a whole new level of creativity.

The key is that we make time for romance. It's very easy for the cares of parenting and earning a living to absorb a husband and wife. Before long, two people who were madly in love a few years before hardly know each other any more. Many times these marriages result in one or both of the partners feeling lonely, trapped, and unfulfilled. From this predicament, the chances of an affair increase.

If you haven't romanced your husband lately, think of something creative and sexy you can do especially for him. Maybe you could kidnap him from work for an evening of excitement. Or arrange for a sitter away from home and meet your man at the door in your most alluring lingerie. Perhaps you could leave a piece of your lingerie in his glove box with a handwritten invitation from you. Make sure to put a sticky note on his steering wheel to tell him to look in the glove box. Use your imagination!

While being a mother is one of the most important things you'll ever do, having a solid and thrilling marriage is just as important. Kids who see their parents madly in love are more likely to grow up and have strong marriages themselves.

SURVIVAL SKILL

Make a list of three things you want your husband to do for you...and do them for him. "So in everything, do to others what you would have them do to you" (Matthew 7:12).

If at first you don't succeed,
you're running about average.

—M.H. ALDERSON

36

To Husband or Not to Husband?

There was also a prophetess, Anna, the daughter of Phanuel,
of the tribe of Asher. She was very old; she had lived with her
husband seven years after her marriage, and then was a widow
until she was eighty-four. She never left the temple but
worshiped night and day, fasting and praying.

LUKE 2:36-37

During a Palm Sunday service at my father's church, I excused myself in the middle of the sermon for a trip to the ladies room. When I returned, I smiled at my husband, Daniel, as he turned his legs to one side so I could reclaim my spot beside him on the pew. Stepping in front of his knees, I glanced down at my grandmother, who sat on the pew in front of us, and admired the way the lights shown past her hairnet and onto her smooth hair, turning it almost blue-black.

Carefully I raised my arm over her head, not wanting to hit her and disturb the rapt attention she bestowed on the minister as he delivered his sermon. Sneaking another lover's smile to my husband, I sat down.

Looking straight toward the pulpit, I had every intention of listening to my father's sermon…but something was wrong with my grandmother.

Her hair! It was standing straight up! Her forever-present hairnet had been keeping it so smooth, so in place. Now her once-neat hair looked like the quills of an angry porcupine. Every strand stood straight out, reaching for the rafters like cotton candy.

I felt something at my arm. As I glanced down, my confusion grew. My husband slowly, deliberately untangled a black, reticulated thing from the button of my wide, lacy cuff. I wondered if I had somehow snared this strange item in the bathroom.

He leaned toward my ear. "It's her hairnet!" he whispered. His green eyes danced with hilarity.

My grandmother turned around, her dark-brown eyes glittering like a mischievous puppy's, her pearly teeth glistening in a special grin just for me. For one split second the years melted away and my 80-year-old grandmother turned into a playful teenager—with porcupine hair.

I had often wondered why she never went without the hairnet. Now I knew! Sniffling, laughter tears stinging my eyes, I handed her the soft hairnet in what seemed like a slow-motion replay. Without her gaze meeting mine again, she took it. Her mouth now set in a fiercely determined line, she methodically replaced the hairnet as if she did this sort of thing in every church service.

The porcupine vanished, leaving the smooth blue-black mane in its place. But for me and my husband—and the back half of the congregation—the porcupine didn't go away. It stubbornly hibernated in our minds, blocking out everything else. I'm guessing no one in those six pews could remember what my father's sermon was about that Sunday. As soon as the last "amen" was uttered, a chorus of laughter burst forth in spontaneous release.

I didn't think guffaws could get any louder until my grandmother said, "I have been sitting up there the whole service wondering why in the world Debra reached up and ripped off my hair."

My poor grandmother actually thought I had nabbed her hairnet on purpose!

I collapsed on a nearby pew and howled with laughter. Ma White got irritated at me for laughing so loudly. She always said I laughed too loudly. But everyone says I have *her* laugh.

Anybody who knew my grandmother would agree that the woman was nothing short of a *force*. If she was in the room, nay, in the same neighborhood, you knew she was present, and you knew *exactly* what she thought, whether or not you wanted her opinion. Part of that was because she did have a strong personality to start with. Then again, I believe much of her strength came from the hardships life dealt her. When my grandmother was in her early forties, her husband left her and her children and divorced her against her will. She was left to support her children on her own. Even though she was highly intelligent, she didn't have an education. That meant she had to take whatever job she could find, using the skills she did have. She was able to secure a position in a sewing factory. This was back in the fifties, so the family barely squeaked by.

To my knowledge my grandmother never allowed herself to have another romantic attachment. When the children were grown and had families of their own, she still didn't get involved with another man. Once a young, single man in his late twenties asked her why she never remarried. She turned that question right around and said, "Why aren't *you* married?" He just laughed in response.

During my childhood, adolescence, and early adulthood, I took my grandmother's singleness for granted. I never really bothered to analyze her married status much. I just accepted that she was Ma White and that she was my single grandmother.

Now that she's gone and I'm older, I look at her choices with some awe. She supported herself and her children during an era when many women didn't work outside the home and the professional world wasn't made to give women a fair shake in salary and benefits. But somehow she managed.

She was an attractive woman who I'm sure had romantic opportunities, but she chose to remain single. I'm positive part of her decision involved the fact that she didn't want to take the chance on another marriage. There was a lot at stake after her divorce, including the well-being of her children.

The world in which we live is full of single moms. Sometimes moms are single because their husbands abandoned their families. Sometimes they're single because they gave birth out-of-wedlock and wisely chose not to have an abortion. And then there are the young widows who are left with children.

Too many times, these single moms might rush into marriages that turn sour for whatever reason. Church pews are now full of mothers who have been married three or four times and the most recent marriages are on the rocks. Even though loneliness is a terrible thing to face, many times it's better for moms with children still at home to emulate my grandmother and remain single. With American news headlines full of stories of stepfathers or boyfriends who have molested or beaten children, I would personally be leery of entering another marriage or serious relationship should I suddenly find myself single.

I'm not saying that God doesn't lead single mothers to marry. There are many stories of stepfathers who have been better to their stepchildren than the biological father ever was. I do believe there are some situations where God has worked to heal people's lives and put people together in a special way. These are the miracle stories we all love to hear about.

However, the single mother who is considering remarrying should make absolutely certain that the pending marriage is God-ordained. It's so easy to misconstrue our own desires as the voice of the Lord. God will not guide us into living out of wedlock with a man just to see if it might work. He will not direct us to marry a man who is already verbally or physically abusing us, threatening our children, or in the throes of substance abuse. Furthermore, if we want husbands because we desperately desire the "happily ever after, Cinderella dream," sometimes it's healthy to allow the dream to die and accept the reality of what's best for us and our children.

Life can be hard. Like my grandmother, everyone doesn't have their romantic dreams fulfilled. If Ma White made it alone in the 50s, you can make it today. There are all sorts of assistance programs now available for single moms. Most cities have one or several food pantries, and many churches have outreaches to single mothers. Even if you don't have an education, there are now programs that provide childcare while you go to college or trade school. You *can* survive on your own!

I've decided if anything happens to my husband, I'm going to be like my grandmother. God's direction to remarry will have to be so strong it will be the equivalent of skywriting. I love my kids too much to take the chance on their being hurt by a possible wrong choice.

If you are in a situation where you need to make a decision, don't jump into any marriage you're uncertain of. Take the time to develop a deep intimacy with God so that every choice you make will be guided by Him and not by human desires or failings.

SURVIVAL SKILL

If you are a single mom struggling to make ends meet, call the Chamber of Commerce in your city and enquire about assistance programs for single mothers. Also ask them for the number of any church alliances in the area. Sometimes one phone call will lead to another and another, and you will find some help. Don't give up!

I am married to me!

—KIM MCLEAN, SINGER,
DOVE AWARD SONGWRITER, SINGLE MOM

37

Your Kids Will
Turn Out All Right—
If You Don't Poison 'Em First

*Do you not know that your body is a temple of the Holy Spirit,
who is in you, whom you have received from God? You are not your own;
you were bought at a price. Therefore honor God with your body.*

1 CORINTHIANS 6:19-20

When Brett was about ten months old, my husband went into his room to change his diaper. Soon he came out with a ghastly look on his face. He held Brett, who didn't look really happy.

"Debra," Daniel said, "Brett has swallowed rubbing alcohol."

"What!" I shrieked. "How did that happen?"

"I don't know. There was a bottle nearby and he got it and the lid was loose."

"Oh my word!"

"He threw up," Daniel explained.

As new parents, we were overly conscientious about *ordinary* stuff. This was enough to send us both through the ceiling. I scurried around in a nervous dither and finally had the presence of mind to find the number for the Poison Hotline. I placed the call and waited for an answer.

The man who came on the line was friendly, supportive, and calm.

I explained exactly what happened and assured the man our son had indeed thrown up.

"He's going to be okay," the man assured. "Since he threw up, his body was essentially getting rid of it. You don't have anything to worry about."

After I hung up and reported the news to my husband, we both wilted with relief. From then on we kept the rubbing alcohol out of reach.

I thought our alcohol story was really bad until I heard from a couple of friends. One friend reported that he had once accidentally given his small child the dog's worm medicine. His wife had left a note that he was supposed to administer the child's liquid medication. The bottles were very similar. My friend picked up the wrong one and gave a teaspoonful to his child.

When he realized his mistake, he called the vet. The vet assured him there would be no damage. His final prognosis was, "Just keep an eye on her and make sure she doesn't start barking."

I also learned of another friend who had an interesting experience with wrong medication. Since she was divorced, she had to send her son to his father's for the weekend. The son was still a preschooler, so the mother included everything she thought he might need for the weekend. That included a medication bag that held the child's medicine and some other important things, such as Ipecac syrup. This is a liquid that induces vomiting in case your child swallows poison or anything else harmful. Yes, years ago the medical profession suggested all parents of young children keep the syrup on hand; now, they're saying it can be more harmful than good. Anyway, the mother gave the father instructions for administering the medicine to the child. He thought he followed her instructions explicitly but started encountering some difficulties.

While talking with his ex-wife he said, "Every time I give him the medicine, he throws up! Have you had that problem?"

She said, "No. That's odd. You are giving him the bottle marked…" and she described the bottle.

He said, "Let me look." He pulled out what he thought was the child's "medicine" and discovered he'd been giving him the substance that induces vomiting.

His ex-wife was *not happy!*

Really, when you consider all the things kids get into, it's a wonder any child lives to adulthood. When I was about five, I used to eat dry Dog Chow. No joke! I'd sneak into the cabinet where the dog food was kept and get a few pieces. I remember to this day that it tasted like cardboard. Why I ate dogfood was anybody's guess. I also recall getting into the refrigerator and pinching off pieces of raw bacon and eating that as well. Yes, raw! I remember my mother catching me in the act. Maybe the diet of Dog Chow and raw bacon explains "the problem" with me now. It's all got to be related somehow.

Aside from my weird diet beginnings, I'm now the mother who reads the fine print on all the medication and foods and drinks. I always question doctors and pharmacists if I have any concerns about the medication prescribed for my children. Sometimes my queries have irritated a few professionals, but I ask anyway. The health of my children is at stake! Every prescription comes with a printout regarding any side effects the medication might cause. Read the print-out! There have been a few times I requested a different medication because I didn't like the side effects of the one I got or because the medication clashed with my child's existing condition, such as asthma.

Then there are the food issues. Hey, if my kids are going to eat "Cat Chow," I want to know what's in it. My sister-in-law once said, "Debra was the one who didn't think she wanted any children, and now she's turned into Mother Superior." That's pretty close to the truth. I'm very concerned about what my kids put into their bodies. Seriously, I don't let them eat Cat Chow. To my knowledge neither of them have even offered to try the stuff.

But when it comes to regular, everyday food, I push fruits and fresh veggies and limit Brett and Brooke's intake of sugar and caffeine. My son has some moderate attention deficit issues. I've looked into all the available medications for attention deficit and decided I didn't like the side effects. Now we're learning to help him manage the problem with alternative options. For instance, I've realized that Brett's attention span goes to zero if he eats sugar. That makes any academic endeavors nearly impossible. I've also learned that if I give Brett caffeinated beverages he goes into orbit and bounces off the walls. Forget studying anything. Brooke, on the other hand, isn't as strongly affected by sugar and caffeine. But caffeine after five in the afternoon does inhibit her ability to fall asleep.

So many kids these days are overcharged with stimulants such as caffeine and sugar and the red dye in foods. Those same kids can be the ones who are put on medication to control hyperactivity or attention deficit. If your child struggles in this area, consider altering his or her diet before trying medication. Or if they're on medication, have a trial one- or two-week period in which you alter the diet and suspend medication (perhaps on spring break or during the summer and with a doctor's approval).

Remember, remove all sugar and caffeine from the diet—especially during the school week. Splenda is a child-approved sugar substitute. Many products such as ice cream and popsicles now use Splenda. You can also buy Stevia, an herbal sweetener that serves as a sugar substitute. Often organic food stores carry Stevia. Don't forget, chocolate does have some caffeine, so a nice cup of sugary hot cocoa on a cold winter's school morning can be a quick trip to hyperactivity and a short attention span. All I would have to do is allow my son to have one regular Coca Cola in the morning before school, and they'd be calling me to come pick him up or put him in a straight jacket.

Brett is off all sugar Monday through Friday. I allow him to have one regular dessert on Saturday and one on Sunday and usually one or two sugary drinks for the whole weekend. It seems there's always something going on at church that involves sugar. I have been amazed at the difference in his ability to pay attention, concentrate, and focus when he's sugar free.

Our whole family has had to adjust to Brett's needs. But that's what being a healthy family is all about; we adjust to meet each other's needs. We don't eat sugar in front of Brett Monday through Friday. I don't buy cereals with high sugar content. (Many popular cereals now have reduced sugar versions.) I also arrange for decaffeinated drinks for him any time we are indulging in caffeinated beverages. Furthermore, I make decaf ice tea for our dinner and sweeten it with Stevia and one scoop of Splenda. Any ice cream we buy is sweetened with Splenda. I've also purchased chocolate syrup with Splenda, so he can make an occasional glass of chocolate milk (not before school time, due to the caffeine). Clever moms can find all sorts of ways to navigate around sugar and caffeine and still have a happy child and family.

SURVIVAL SKILL

The Poison Center Hotline is 1-800-222-1222.

Being a good mother involves adjusting our cooking and pantries to meet our kids' needs.

38

What's Cookin'?

A wife of noble character who can find?…She makes linen garments and sells them, and supplies the merchants with sashes.

PROVERBS 31:10,24

Gail Gaymer Martin grew up in a time when wearing brand-name clothes wasn't heard of in the average home. People were grateful to have a couple pairs of shoes. Sunday dinner meant the whole family sitting around the dining room table enjoying a roast beef or roasted stuffed chicken. But times have certainly changed. Today, brand names can be a must and for some eating Sunday dinner together is a lost art. Today's teenagers…and even younger children…wouldn't think of wearing hand-me-downs or turning mom's old dress into a skirt. Designer clothes and fast food are a way of life.

One thing Gail remembers back in those special days is the way her parents made things last. Worn-down heels went to the shoemaker. Her father's woolen sweater, shrunk in the wash, was shifted to the eight-year-old's closet. Gail recalls when one of her favorite skirts became faded and her mom came home from the store with a box of bright blue dye.

"What's this for?" Gail asked. While holding the packet in her hand, she was already guessing.

"I'm going to dye your skirt. It'll look like new," her mother replied.

It won't to me, Gail thought, but back then kids didn't sass parents.

So she watched her mom put the large roaster pan on the stove, heat the water, add the dye, and drop in her skirt. Disappointed, Gail walked away.

The next day when she came home from school, her mom had dried and ironed the dyed skirt. To Gail's surprise, her mother had been correct. The skirt looked new! She wore it to church a couple of Sunday's later and wondered if anyone would realize it was her old skirt. No one did.

That same afternoon, Gail and her family sat in the house smelling the wonderful roast beef her mom was preparing for Sunday dinner. They looked forward to the Sunday meals because they were fancier than the weekdays'. During the week, meals often consisted of chipped beef, macaroni and cheese, and salmon patties with creamed peas.

This Sunday potatoes and carrots were boiling on the stove and her mother's homemade bread was sliced and waiting on the table with a crisp salad. The wonderful aroma drew the family to the kitchen and caused them to salivate as they waited until mom lifted the lid of the roasting pan. Finally the moment arrived. Gail's mother lifted the lid, and the family's mouths dropped open. The roast beef was always brown, succulent, and melt-in-your-mouth tender, but this one appeared to be from someone else's kitchen. The pot roast was the exact shade of Gail's new skirt—bright blue!

"What in the world?" her father questioned. "What's wrong with the roast?"

Gail's mom looked at Gail, and she looked down at her bright blue skirt.

"I used the roaster to dye Gail's skirt," her mother said. "I thought I scrubbed it out really well."

Needless to say, the family didn't have roast beef that Sunday afternoon, and her mother got a new roaster.[1]

What are your cooking skills like? Do you enjoy cooking, or would you rather not? Some people seem born to cook, others can't boil water without burning it.

While I don't enjoy sewing, I'm one of those born to cook. My first efforts were in the third grade when I made a carrot cake all by myself. The dessert turned out great! From those humble beginnings, I grew into a young wife who loved a new and challenging recipe. In the twenty-three years Daniel and I have been married, I have created only a few culinary failures. Fortunately, none have been blue. One of the failures involved an orange curry chicken recipe during the first year of our marriage. We still talk about how perfectly awful that dish was and both agree it was just a bad recipe.

We were married ten-and-a-half years before we had our first child. During those years, I spent hours and hours in the kitchen. Many Sundays we enjoyed homemade yeast rolls and all sorts of other mouth-watering treats. I created numerous yummy dishes that made even our friends marvel. After eating one of my pies with, yes, a homemade crust, one retired churchman even claimed, "You just don't find many young women these days who can cook like Debra does. Most young women can't make pie crust like that." I discreetly glowed with pride—if you can call the equivalent of red flashing lights "discreet glowing."

Then I had my son. What a challenge! His presence cut my kitchen time in half. Nevertheless, I was still a committed cooker.

When we adopted our daughter from Vietnam, my writing career was beginning to explode. What a change in my kitchen life! Who has time to spend hours on one dessert or one meal when you've got toddlers hanging onto your legs and a 300-page book to write in six weeks? Forget homemade crust and yeast rolls and beautiful dishes. I seriously doubt my family would have even *noticed* if I cooked a *blue* pot roast. We'd have been so glad to see a roast that we'd have eaten the thing whether it was blue or polka dotted.

Because writing opportunities have grown into the fulfillment of God-given dreams, I have made my choices. While my husband and I make sure our family shares regular meal times together, we sometimes go to the deli and buy chicken, cole slaw, and potato salad. Sometimes we prepare frozen entrées from the grocery store or we grab burgers on the way home. And my husband often grills.

Our family has joyfully made many other adjustments as well. I do still cook, but I've gleaned new, short-cut skills in the kitchen. My favorite recipes have become the easiest ones. My husband has become our dessert man. We've dubbed him our "cookie monster." My son is following in his footsteps. Both the guys in the Smith household genuinely love to cook all sorts of desserts. Now, my *husband* is the one who everybody's bragging about at family gatherings and church events. Furthermore, I have learned the art of buying premade pie crusts, or better yet, shopping the marked down rack at the department store bakery. Just last week I bought four cherry pies, a lemon cake, and a chocolate cake all at 40 percent off. I brought them home and froze them. The next time our church enjoys lunch together and Daniel isn't in "cookie monster" mode, I will take one of those frozen masterpieces.

Sometimes God opens extraordinary opportunities—even for mothers. He certainly has for me. In the face of these opportunities, I would have been out of God's perfect will if I had turned them down because I was convinced that if I didn't align myself with the 1950s American model God would be angry. What I've found is that God's presence is with us when we eat together as a family, whether I bought the chicken at the deli or cooked it on my own rotisserie.

My husband and I have an agreement. When I'm under a book deadline, he's the meal master. He's thrilled to do this because my writing income has freed him to pursue his dreams of a home-based business and given us a flexible schedule so he can travel with me as a ministry partner.

As I work on finishing this chapter, it's dinnertime. My husband has just come in and said, "What do we have that I can grill?" Before I answered, he continued, "I don't know…maybe I'd rather fix Hamburger Helper."

No, I'm no longer acting like a gourmet chef. But I am impacting readers, and lives are being changed. While I haven't sacrificed my family, I have sacrificed my pursuit of creative cooking. Every time a new book releases, I feel the warmth of God's smile.

SURVIVAL SKILL

Any time you accidentally wash a dark item of clothing with whites and turn everything pink, pale blue, or some other color, use Rit Color Remover to remove the new tint. Rit Color Remover can be found in fabric stores and some drug or department stores.

Wise mothers celebrate their strongest skills and don't fret over the things they aren't good at.

Kitchen Signs

Although you'll find our house a mess, come in, sit down, converse. It doesn't always look like this: Some days it's even worse.

I came, I saw, I decided to order take out.

If you write in the dust, please don't date it!

If you don't like my standards of cooking...lower your standards.

Martha Stewart doesn't live here!

A balanced diet is a cookie in each hand!

My life is filled with romance, danger, love... and dust balls the size of cattle.

I clean house every other day. Today is the other day.

A messy kitchen is a happy kitchen, and this kitchen is delirious.

Thou shalt not weigh more than thy refrigerator.

Ring bell for maid service. If no answer, do it yourself!

I would cook dinner, but I can't find the can opener!

So this isn't "Home Sweet Home"...ADJUST!

I'd live life in the fast lane, but I'm married to a speed bump.

Countless numbers of people have eaten in this kitchen and gone on to lead normal lives.

My next house will have no kitchen... just vending machines.

My house was clean last week... too bad you missed it!

39

Kitchen Shortcuts and Easy Recipes

Baked Potatoes in Crock-Pot

This is a great way to have baked potatoes ready for after church or after work.

- Wrap Irish potatoes or sweet potatoes in aluminum foil.
- Place them in the slow cooker or Crock-Pot.
- Cook on high for 3 to 4 hours, depending on number of potatoes.
- Cook on low for 6 to 8 hours, depending on number of potatoes.[1]

Banana Nut Bread

This is a good recipe to use when your bananas are too ripe to be eaten. Even if you don't need the bread that day, you can freeze it for later use.

Ingredients

⅓ cup vegetable oil
3 large bananas, mashed
2½ cups Bisquick
½ tsp. vanilla
3 eggs
1 cup sugar or Splenda
⅔ cup chopped pecans

Directions
- Mix all ingredients.

- Spray two loaf pans with cooking oil or olive oil.

- Pour mixture into pans and bake at 350 degrees for 55 minutes.

- Cool 5 minutes before turning out.

- If freezing, cool completely before wrapping for freezer.

- Tastes great hot with butter or margarine.

Bubbles

Ingredients
¼ cup dish detergent
1 cup water
1 to 2 tsp. sugar

Directions
- Mix and enjoy blowing bubbles.

- The sugar is what makes them work.

Cake Mix Cookies

Ingredients
1 box cake mix (any flavor)
1 cup cooking oil
1 egg
Optional: ½ cup finely chopped pecans

Directions
- Mix ingredients together.

- Press into large cookie sheet with ledge or large baking pan.

- Bake 10 to 12 minutes at 325 degrees.

• While still warm cut into squares.

See "Easy Shape Cookies" (page 200) for using this recipe to make shape cookies.[2]

Chicken Enchiladas

This recipe has been in our family since I was a small child. It's my all-time favorite casserole.

Ingredients

1 chicken or 6 chicken breasts, cooked and deboned, or 4 to 6 cans of canned chicken, or enough to have the same amount as a whole chicken

1 medium-sized bag Doritoes or any plain tortilla chips

1 can diced, green chilies

1 medium onion, diced

1 stick butter or margarine

2 cups shredded cheddar cheese (I *always* buy the large bag of generic-brand, preshredded cheese. This saves lots of time.)

3 cans cream of chicken soup

Directions

• Cook chicken by boiling, pressure cooking, or placing in Crock-Pot on low all day.

• Debone chicken.

• If using canned chicken, no preparation needed.

• Sauté onion and green chilies in butter until onions are clear.

• Add cream of chicken soup. Stir until blended.

• Add chicken. Stir until blended.

• Pour Doritoes into long casserole dish.

- Pour chicken mixture on top of Doritoes.

- Top with shredded cheese.

- Bake at 350 degrees for 20 to 30 minutes, until cheese is melted and the corners are bubbly.

Chicken Wings Extraordinaire

This is a quick and easy way to make "fried chicken" without the mess of frying. It's also lower in fat.

Ingredients
Chicken wings, thawed
Bisquick
Salt and pepper to taste

Directions
- Salt and pepper chicken wings.

- Roll wings in Bisquick. Place in baking pan.

- Bake at 350 degrees until golden brown, about 1 hour.

Cobbler to Die For

Ingredients
1 large can of fruit, cherries, or berries of your choice (I usually use peaches), or cut up fresh fruit of your choice
⅓ cup margarine
1¼ cup sugar or Splenda
¾ cup flour
¾ cup milk
2 tsps. baking powder

Directions

- Mix fruit with ½ cup of sugar or Splenda and set aside.

- Melt margarine in pan.

- Mix ¾ cup sugar, flour, and milk to create batter. Pour into melted margarine.

- Pour fruit into batter. Do not stir. This will look messy and you'll be tempted to think you've made a mistake. You haven't!

- Bake at 350 degrees for 1 hour. The fruit sinks to the bottom. The dough rises to the top.

- Serve hot with ice cream.

Corn They'll Remember

Ingredients

1 to 2 cans of corn or bags of frozen corn (frozen is my favorite)
½ to ¾ stick of butter
⅛ to ¼ cup of sugar or Splenda
Salt and pepper to taste

Directions

- Place corn in iron skillet. If using frozen corn, add ½ cup of water per bag of corn.

- Add the other ingredients.

- Turn burner on highest heat.

- Cook until the corn starts sizzling—until all the water is gone and only butter remains.

- Serve hot.

Dump Cake

Ingredients

1 can cherry pie filling (or other fruit)
1 can crushed pineapple
2 sticks margarine or butter
1 yellow cake mix
1 to 2 cups chopped pecans or nuts of choice (The more
   nuts the better!)
Optional: 3½ oz. coconut

Directions

• Use a 13 x 9 inch pan.

• Spoon cherry pie filling along the bottom of the pan.

• Layer pineapple with juice on top of pie filling.

• Sprinkle yellow cake mix on top of pineapple.

• Cut margarine/butter in squares and cover top of
  cake mix. Or melt the butter and drizzle on top of the
  cake mix.

• Top with pecans or nuts of choice.

• Optional: Top with coconut.

• Bake at 325 degrees for 1 hour.

Easy Shape Cookies

When my son was three, he wanted to make shape
cookies. By the time I got all the ingredients out and was
halfway through mixing the dough, Brett said he was
tired of making cookies. So I was left with a mound of
cookie dough, a horrid mess, and a bored three-year-old.
I finished making the cookies, but I decided there had to
be a better and quicker way. They say necessity is the
mother of invention. The following is what I invented.

Directions

• Prepare "Cake Mix Cookies" (see page 196).*

• Immediately after baking and while baked cookie dough is still hot in the pan, don't cut it into squares. Instead, press cookie cutters into the dough like you would if you were pressing them into raw cookie dough.

• Depending on the size of the cookie cutters, you should be able to make 6 to 15 shape cookies per sheet of square cooked dough.

• Allow the cookies to cool. Once they cool, punch cookies out as you would paper dolls.

Kids love the cookie shapes. Dads love the scraps. Moms-on-the-go love the whole process because it takes only 30 minutes to complete and doesn't make a huge mess.

* You may substitute store-bought or homemade sugar cookie dough, but the cake mix cookies are the easiest to punch out after they've cooled because they are very crisp.

Fruit Pizza

This is a great way to get kids to eat fresh fruit and berries.

Ingredients

1 tube sugar cookie dough
1 8-oz. package cream cheese
¼ cup sugar or Splenda
Strawberries, grapes, and blueberries—as much as desired.

Directions

• Divide cookie dough and press over bottom of two round pizza pans.

- Bake at 350 degrees approximately 10 minutes or until brown.
- Allow to cool. Move to large plate or serving board.
- Mix cream cheese with sugar or Splenda.
- Spread cream cheese mixture over both large cookies.
- Cover with sliced strawberries, sliced or whole grapes, and blueberries.[3]

Green Beans They'll Remember

Option 1
Ingredients
1 to 2 cans green beans or 1 to 2 bags frozen beans
Strips of uncooked bacon
Bacon grease (optional)
Garlic salt

Note: For lower calorie green beans, leave out bacon and bacon grease and simply use garlic salt.

Directions
- Place beans in a medium-sized sauce pan. If using frozen beans, add ½ cup of water per bag.
- Place several slices of bacon in the beans.
- Add bacon grease if desired (this ups the cholesterol count).
- Add garlic salt to taste.
- Cook on high until ¾ of the liquid is gone from the beans.

Option 2
Ingredients
1 to 2 cans green beans or 1 to 2 bags frozen green beans

⅛ to ¼ cup cooking oil
1⁄16 to ⅛ cup sugar or Splenda
Salt to taste

Directions

- Place beans in medium-sized sauce pan. If using frozen beans, add ½ cup water per bag.

- Add rest of ingredients.

- Cook on medium to high heat until almost all the juice is gone.

- Beans will look shiny because of the oil.

Grilled Potatoes

Ingredients
Potatoes, sliced like thick potato chips
Butter to taste
Salt, pepper, or powdered ranch dressing mix

Directions

- While grilling meat, you can also cook your potatoes.

- Place the thick potato slices on the grill, brush them with butter, sprinkle with salt and pepper or powdered ranch dressing mix.

- Turn as needed. Cook until done.[4]

Hamburger Patties

Buy hamburger meat in bulk. Shape into individual patties. I often use a small saucer as a "mold" for hamburger patties. Just mash the hamburger patty onto the saucer. When you cover the saucer with the meat to desired thickness, you've got a nearly perfect round patty. Freeze patties on cookie sheets. When frozen, use a spatula to pop the patties off the cookie sheet, place them in freezer bags, and store in the freezer.[5]

Lemonade Pie

Ingredients
1 can Eagle Brand condensed milk
1 small can frozen lemonade
1 8-oz. container Cool Whip
1 graham cracker pie crust
½ cup chopped nuts, optional

Directions
• Mix condensed milk and thawed lemonade.

• Fold in Cool Whip and pour into pie crust.

• Top with nuts.

• Chill.

Oriental Cole Slaw

1 lb. shredded cabbage (or buy preshredded cabbage at the grocery store)
1 to 4 green onions, chopped
2 pkgs. chicken ramen noodles
⅓ cup vinegar
½ cup sugar or Splenda
¼ cup vegetable oil
1 cup slivered almonds
1 cup sunflower seeds
Dash of salt

Directions
• Mix cabbage and green onions.

• Take the 2 pkgs. of ramen noodle chicken flavoring and mix with sugar, vinegar, oil, and dash of salt.

- Pour dressing over greens and mix well.
- Chill approximately 2 hours.
- Just before serving, add almonds, sunflower seeds, and noodles.

Optional: Before adding almonds and sunflower seeds, spray a cookie sheet with vegetable oil and lightly toast the nuts and seeds at 350 degrees for 8 to 10 minutes.

Peanut Brittle Perfecto

Ingredients
1 cup Karo syrup
1 cup water
1 cup sugar
Dash of salt
1 cup raw peanuts
1 tbsp. butter or margarine
1 tsp. baking soda

Directions
- Place a cast iron skillet over highest heat setting on stove top.
- Mix Karo syrup, water, sugar, and salt. Pour mixture into skillet.
- Boil until the mixture begins to thicken.
- Drop a dot of the mixture into a cup of cool water. If you can form a soft ball with your fingers, it's time to pour in the peanuts.
- Stir in 1 cup raw peanuts.
- Add 1 heaping tablespoon of butter or margarine.
- Stir until the foam turns to light golden. You will hear the peanuts popping as you stir.

- Stir in 1 heaping teaspoon of baking soda.

- Immediately pour into a greased pie pan or cookie sheet. If using pie pans, you will need two.

- Allow to harden and then break into pieces.[6]

Pizza in a Minute

Ingredients
Flour tortillas or canned biscuits
Pizza sauce
Shredded cheese—cheddar, mozzarella, or Velveeta

Optional: Any other pizza toppings you have such as bell peppers, onions, finely chopped spinach, pepperoni. (This is a good place to sneak spinach in your kids' diet.)

Directions
- If using canned biscuits, press biscuits out with fingertips directly on cookie sheet until the biscuit is thin and looks like a small pizza crust.

- If using tortillas, lay them out on the cookie sheet.

- Spoon pizza sauce over flour tortilla or pressed out biscuits.

- Top with cheese and favorite toppings.

- Bake at 350 degrees for 8 to 10 minutes.

Note: When using flour tortillas, you can place pizza sauce on $\frac{1}{2}$ of the tortilla, add cheese and any other toppings, and then fold the tortilla in half. This makes a "pizza pocket." I often serve pizza pockets to my kids and their friends during the summer.

Pot Roast Exellente

Ingredients

Roast of your choice
2 envelopes onion soup mix

Directions

- Place roast in baking dish.

- Pour dry onion soup mix into bottom of pan.

- Add 2 to 3 cups of water.

- Optional: Include vegetables such as peeled carrots and potatoes.

- Cover with aluminum foil.

- Bake at 350 degrees for 4 hours.

Play Clay

Ingredients

1 cup flour
1 tbsp. vegetable oil
1 cup water
½ cup salt
2½ tsp. cream of tartar
Food coloring

Note: May add glitter, vanilla flavoring, cinnamon, or any fruit flavor such as strawberry. Because the flavoring is used for scent only, you may also add potpourri oil or liquid. Make sure young children know not to eat the scented clay.

Directions

- Mix all ingredients.

- Heat in sauce pan, stirring constantly until a ball is formed.

- If adding glitter, mix in at this point and kneed play clay until evenly distributed.

This has the same texture as Play Dough. I made Play Clay at a Valentine's party for my kids and their guests without the glitter or scent. I allowed the children to help make the red play clay. We divided it out so each child got a nice-sized chunk of play clay. They played with it during the party. Then we used ziplock bags for them to take home their play clay. The whole project was a *huge* hit! Surprisingly, it didn't make that big of a mess.

Potato Casserole

Ingredients

1 to 2 bags frozen, loose hash browns. These are essentially frozen shredded potatoes, loose in the package.

Cooking oil spray

½ to 1 cup chopped fresh onions or may substitute dried onions at half these proportions

Garlic salt to taste

¼ to ½ cup of milk

½ to 1 stick of butter or margarine

8 to 16 oz. sour cream (optional)

Shredded cheddar cheese or you may substitute Velveeta Cheese

Directions

- Spray medium-sized pan with cooking oil spray.

- Empty bag(s) of shredded potatoes into pan.

- Pour in milk.

- Top with garlic salt to taste. A light sprinkle across the entire surface is usually sufficient. Be careful not to over salt.

- Slice butter. Place across the top of the potatoes.

- Spread sour cream on top until the potatoes are covered nicely.
- Cover with foil. Bake at 350 degrees for 40 to 45 minutes.
- Remove from oven. Add a generous layer of shredded cheese or Velveeta.
- Place uncovered dish back in oven.
- Bake at 350 degrees for 10 to15 minutes.

Pressure Cookers

Pressure Cookers are a great cooking tool and especially helpful for working moms. In 30 minutes you can cook a melt-in-your-mouth roast. In 15 to 30 minutes you can cook a whole chicken or chicken parts until they are falling off the bone. Pressure cookers are excellent for quickly cooking potatoes for mashing, dried beans, and smothered steak.

Ranch Style Salad

This recipe has been in my family since I was a child. It's an excellent complement to the Chicken Enchiladas found on page 197.

Ingredients
½ to 1 head of lettuce, depending on desired size of salad
½ to 1 can ranch-style beans
8 to 16 oz. shredded cheddar cheese
½ bag to 1 bag Fritos
¼ to ½ medium-sized onion
½ to 1 tomato, diced
½ to 1 bottle Catalina Dressing

Directions

Crunch up Fritos. Mix all ingredients. Serve as soon as fixed. This salad does not chill well (the chips get soggy). Make as much as you think will serve your family for one meal. Remember, if you use the recipe with one head of lettuce, you'll have enough to feed 8 to 10 people. This is one of those recipes that grows as you make it.

Smoothies

The key to the most successful smoothies is using *frozen* fruit.

Option 1
Ingredients

8-oz. container yogurt (choose any flavor, nonfat, low carb, or regular)
½ cup frozen fruit to match the yogurt
1 tsp. vanilla
Honey, sugar, or Splenda to taste

Directions

• Combine ingredients in a blender or food processor.

• Pour into glass and enjoy.[7]

Option 2
Ingredients

1 to 3 cups frozen berries of your preference (we use strawberries, blueberries, and raspberries)
¼ to ½ cup milk (low fat, nonfat, or whole milk)
Sugar, honey, or Splenda to taste

Directions

• Blend in food processor until smooth. Dip out and serve in a bowl.

• This smoothie has a soft ice cream or sherbet consistency. Kids love it!

Note: My son is 11 and frequently makes his own smoothies. Smoothies are a great way to get kids to eat fresh fruit and berries.

Spinach They'll Love

Ingredients

1 to 2 bags frozen spinach
1 to 2 8-oz. packages cream cheese
Garlic powder and salt to taste
Optional: Pepper to taste

Directions

• Cook spinach in microwave until thawed.

• Drain spinach and use paper towel to absorb excess water.

• Chop cream cheese into small chunks and stir into spinach.

• Add salt and garlic powder to taste.

• Microwave 1½ to 2 minutes until the mixture is able to be stirred smoothly.

• Serve hot.[8]

Squash and Rice Casserole

Ingredients

1 cup rice
2 to 4 squash, zucchini or yellow, chopped into small, thin pieces about the size of a nickel
1 pkg. dry onion soup mix
3 cups water

Directions

• Place all ingredients in a small casserole dish.

• Bake at 350 degrees for 1 to 1½ hours.

• Serve hot.

Sweet Potatoes

Ingredients

4 large sweet potatoes
¼ cup sugar or Splenda to taste
½ stick butter or margarine
½ tsp. salt to taste
2 tbsps. cinnamon to taste

Directions

• Cook sweet potatoes in Crock-Pot as directed on
  page 195 or bake them in the oven until soft.

• Remove foil and skins from potatoes.

• Mash sweet potatoes using large fork or potato
  masher. If you bake them long enough, they'll be
  very soft and easy to mash.

• Add butter, cinnamon, sugar, and salt.

• Stir until blended and butter is melted. Serve hot.

This dish reheats nicely for leftovers. I often make enough
for two meals.

Thousand Island Salad Dressing

Mix 2 parts Miracle Whip to 1 part ketchup.

You can also add the following if you like:
    1 to 2 tsps. lemon juice
    1 to 2 tsps. dried, diced onions

1 to 2 tsps. sweet pickle relish
Dash of garlic salt
Dash of parsley
Dash of chili powder

Tortilla Rolls

Ingredients
1 pkg. flour tortillas (any size)
2 pkgs. cream cheese
1 pkg. Hidden Valley Original Dry Ranch Dressing
1 small can chopped olives
1 small jar pimentos
Sour cream
Dash of salt

Directions
• Let cream cheese soften at room temperature.

• Add 2 tbsp. of sour cream.

• Mix until creamy.

• Add dry ranch dressing, drained black olives, and drained pimentos.

• Mix well.

• Spread a thin layer over tortilla, all the way to edges.

• Add a clump to one side and start rolling the tortilla over the clump. This creates a center, thick with filling.

• Let chill in an air-tight container for 1 hour.

• Cut into slices with electric knife or sharp knife. The rolls will look a little like cinnamon rolls.

40

Internet Resources

Support for Christian Moms

Brenda Nixon. www.brendanixon.com. Brenda is the author of *Parenting Power in the Early Years*. She is a mothering expert who offers sound advice. Her website features helpful mom links as well as other supportive information.

Christian Internet Moms. www.christianinternetmoms.net features a weekly radio show by Debra White Smith. This site is a great place to meet other moms and find support from those who are in the throes of parenting.

Christian Mommies. www.christianmommies.com has an extensive selection of articles and resources for single moms.

Christian Parent. www.christianparent.com is a great resource for activities for kids—toddlers to teens. It also features recipes, holiday planners, and much more.

Christian Work-at-Home Moms. At www.cwahm.com you can explore work-at-home opportunities and connect with other moms who have home-based businesses.

Household Hints, Recipes, and Activities

Amy's Kitchen. www.amyskitchen.com offers great, healthy alternatives for delicious kid foods such as pizzas, pizza rolls, toaster pops, and enchiladas.

Between Friends. www.betweenfriends.org offers household hints, time tips, organization suggestions, business ideas, and also has a section for working moms.

Cooks.com. www.cooks.com is a great site that offers innumerable recipes for everything from squash to casseroles to tater tots. The site has different pages for Potluck, New Recipes, Diet/Health Report, Nutrition Facts, and a Conversion Calculator. Also you can do a search for whatever ingredient you want to use, such as chicken, and pull up enough recipes for an army.

Food Fun and Facts. www.foodfunandfacts.com is an intriguing site that lists great household hints, kids cooking and kids crafts, natural skin care, parenting tips, easy recipes, herbal remedies, and recipes from the 1800s.

Kitchen Crafts & More. www.kitchencraftsnmore.net/home.html features over 70 tips for using vinegar and a variety of uses for baking soda. It also offers household and cleaning recipes, clothing care, automotive care, and pet tips.

Recipe Goldmine. This is my favorite domestic website. Visit www.recipegoldmine.com for a phenomenal collection of excellent recipes and household advice. Features: Name-Brand Recipes (such as my husband's Sarah Lee Cheesecake recipe that makes me howl), Sugar Free Recipes, Kitchen Hints, Beauty Recipes, Home Remedies, Household Recipes, Gardening, Crafts, Games, and Free Baking Manuals.

Bearhaus.com. www.bearhaus.com/hints.html features unusual and effective uses for Alka Seltzer, including unclogging a sink drain and cleaning a coffee pot. It also lists all sorts of general household tips, oven-cleaning tips, and kitchen and laundry advice. Furthermore, you can learn about gardening and bugs as well as first aid.

Medical Information

Any time a member of our family is manifesting symptoms that I don't know the origins of, I go on the internet and do some research. If you already have an existing diagnosis, type in the diagnosis on the internet. You'll be amazed at all the correct information that is available.

If you have symptoms you are curious about, the following are a couple of sites you might find helpful. As you surf the net for medical information, be aware that no website should substitute for a physician's care.

Web MD. www.webmd.com. An RN friend recommended this site. I've used it several times and have been very pleased with the information and accuracy.

My Symptoms. www.mysymptoms.net. This is an informative site that gives you medical information about symptoms you are having. It also lists the varying symptoms of different conditions such as heart attacks.

Save a Little Life. www.savealittlelife.com is an excellent website for parents of small children. This site offers safety advice as well as information on CPR classes.

Romance and Marriage

Les and Leslie Parrott. www.realrelationships.com is the home page for the Parrotts. They offer balanced teaching, great books, and great advice!

Pam and Bill Farrell. www.masterfulliving.com offers fun and informative books for those trying to figure out the opposite sex and for people who want to make their marriages better.

Romancing Your Marriage. www.debrawhitesmith.com offers a section of marriage books by me and others, as well as romance novelties especially for married people.

Shopping and Bargains

Coupons. www.couponing.about.com offers printable coupons, bargains, coupon codes, and a free buyer's guide.

Discount and Bargains. www.discountandbargains.com.

eBay. www.ebay.com. eBay is like a huge, online garage sale. I've purchased many items from eBay and have had an overall satisfactory experience. This website allows you to bid on items as well as immediately buy things. Many people I know have saved hundreds of dollars on everything from computer equipment to above-ground pools.

Overstock.com. www.overstock.com is a liquidation spot for many name-brand items that retailers need to clear out of inventory. You can find some really good deals if you shop smart.

Sav-on-Closeouts. www.sav-on-closeouts.com is not to be confused with the Save On Office Supply chain. This website offers an amazing selection of items for pennies. Many items are ideal for Vacation Bible School, children's church, or homeschool crafts. There are also party supplies, holiday items, jewelry, books, candles, gift bags, inflatables, balls, banners, and candy. They also feature some watches.

Travelocity. www.travelocity.com. Any time I need plane tickets, I usually wind up buying them from Travelocity. I've found that, overall, they offer the cheapest tickets. They also have great deals on combination airfare, car rental, and hotel packages.

Notes

Chapter 2

1. *Church Around the World*, church bulletin insert, published by Tyndale House, September 1998.

Chapter 10

1. Martha Rogers, squirrel story. Used by permission.

Chapter 12

1. Alicia Johnson, washing machine story. Used by permission.

Chapter 13

1. Gail Sattler, degu story. Used by permission.

Chapter 15

1. Gail Sattler, dog story. Used by permission.

Chapter 16

1. Kim Sawyer, skunk story. Used by permission.

Chapter 18

1. Judy Cornelia Pearson and Paul Edward Nelson, *Understanding and Sharing* (Dubuque, Iowa: William C. Brown, 1979), p. 50.

Chapter 21

1. Frieda Scully, longhorn story. Used by permission.

Chapter 29

1. Robin Lee Hatcher, snake story. Used by permission.

2. Joy Anderson, rattlesnake story. Used by permission.

Chapter 32

1. *Reflecting God Study Bible, NIV,* notes on Proverbs 13:24, Kenneth Barker, gen. ed. (Grand Rapids, MI: Zondervan Publishing House, 2000), p. 957.

2. Ibid., notes on Psalm 23:4, p. 800.

Chapter 38

1. Gail Gaymer Martin, cooking story. Used by permission.

Chapter 39

1. Betty Crim, *Baked Potatoes in Crock-Pot.* Used by permission.

2. Loretta Gray, *Cake Mix Cookies.* Used by permission.

3. Joy Anderson, *Fruit Pizza.* Used by permission.

4. Betty Crim, *Grilled Potatoes.* Used by permission.

5. Ibid., *Hamburger Patties.* Used by permission.

6. Barbara Langford, *Peanut Brittle.* Used by permission.

7. Brenda Nixon, *Smoothies.* Used by permission.

8. Joy Anderson, *Spinach.* Used by permission.

For more information on
Debra and her ministry, contact:

Real Life Ministries
P.O. Box 1482
Jacksonville, TX 75766

or visit

www.debrawhitesmith.com

Romancing Your Husband

BY DEBRA WHITE SMITH

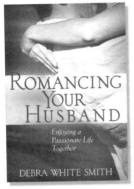

Early days in a relationship are exhilarating, but they can't touch the thrilling love affair you can have now. Cutting through traditional misconceptions and exploring every facet of the Bible's message on marriage, *Romancing Your Husband* reveals how you can create a union others only dream about. From making Jesus an active part of your marriage to arranging fantastic romantic interludes, you'll discover how to—

- make romance a reality
- "knock your husband's socks off"
- become a lover-wife, not a mother-wife
- find freedom in forgiving
- cultivate a sacred romance with God.

Experience fulfillment through romancing your husband...and don't be surprised when he romances you back!

Romancing Your Wife

BY DEBRA WHITE SMITH AND DANIEL W. SMITH

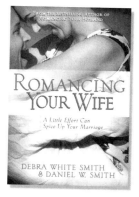

Do you want your husband to surprise you and put more romance in your relationship? *Romancing Your Wife* can help! Give this book to your hubby, and he'll discover ways to create an exciting, enthusiastic marriage.

Debra and her husband, Daniel, offer biblical wisdom and practical advice that when put into practice will help your husband mentally, emotionally, and physically improve his relationship with you. He'll discover tools to build a dynamite marriage, including how to—

- communicate his love more effectively

- make you feel cherished

- better understand your needs and wants

- create a unity of spirit and mind

- increase the passion in your marriage

From insights on little things that jazz up a marriage to more than 20 "Endearing Encounters," *Romancing Your Wife* sets the stage for love and romance.

Great Fiction by Debra White Smith

THE AUSTEN SERIES

First Impressions

Central Park

Reason & Romance

Northpointe Chalet

THE SEVEN SISTERS SERIES/ SISTERS SUSPENSE SERIES

Second Chances

The Awakening/Picture Perfect

A Shelter in the Storm

To Rome with Love

For Your Eyes Only

This Time Around

Let's Begin Again

HARVEST HOUSE PUBLISHERS